I0113664

OF WHOM WE'RE BORN

RACE AND FAMILY

SIMON LENNON

Of Whom We're Born: Race and Family
Non-fiction
Demography, Discrimination
A book in the collection: The West
A book in the series: Identity
Published by Pine Hill Books
Copyright © 2015, 2019, 2025 by Simon Lennon.
All rights reserved.
This book or any portion thereof may not be reproduced, stored in or introduced into a retrieval system, or transmitted in any form or by any means whatsoever (electronic, mechanical, photocopying, recording, or otherwise) without the express written prior permission of the author and the publisher, except for the use of brief quotations in a book review, scholarly journal, or student assignment.
The author asserts his moral rights.
ISBN 978-1-925446-01-2 (electronic)
ISBN 978-1-925446-15-9 (paperback)
52,000 words, plus bibliography, references to 55,000 words
Cover image: The author's youngest son

In memory of my mother

CONTENTS

1. THE POLITICISATION OF SCIENCE

We presume our rejection of racism is the result of research or discoveries amidst our endless enlightenment: a drawing back of past curtains from our minds. It's not. It's a specific Western response to historical events. Ours is the era post Holocaust: the Jewish Holocaust during World War II. We're simply another passage of history.

In 1943, a Polish Jew devised a word that would, for the West, become synonymous with race: genocide. Raphael Lemkin coined the word responding not just to the Holocaust but also the Armenian Genocide by Turks almost thirty years earlier. The carnage European peoples suffered at the Somme, Stalingrad, and elsewhere made the two world wars much like genocide. The Greek word *"genos,"* from which Lemkin derived his word, encompasses family and race: those to whom we were born.

Races, like families, are biological relationships between people: connectedness. The problem, people decided after two world wars and the Holocaust, is that anything linking us together divides us from others.

Nazi dictator Adolf Hitler was no scientist. The Holocaust would still have occurred if there'd been no science of race. There was more than enough anti-Semitic material unrelated to science for him not to need science as a justification. He exploited scientific learning for political objectives.

So do we. Established within months after the end of World War II, the United Nations Educational, Scientific, and Cultural Organisation's principal objective wasn't education, science, or culture. It was the manipulation of them for political objectives. *"The preamble of Unesco's Constitution, adopted in 1945, specifically named racism as one of the social evils which the new Organisation was called upon to combat,"* declared UNESCO in its Publication 791 of 1950.

We think racism is irrational because we think race is irrational, but we don't work so hard against it for being irrational.

1

UNESCO's Constitution blamed World War II on "*the doctrine of inequality of men and races,*" as we did with the Holocaust in mind, although almost universal recognition of racial inequality hadn't driven countries other than Germany or Japan to war.

In fact, World War II owed as much to desires for equality as feelings of inequality. Feeling injustice at the Treaty of Versailles stripping her of land and soul in 1919, Germany's yearning to be treated as the equals of France and Britain facilitated the rise of Nazism in the first place.

No kind of phobia, Nazi Germany shared her sense of racial superiority with the British, Dutch, and Scandinavians, which doesn't make us investigate Nazi thinking. It serves only to lump us accidental accomplices together.

Repulsed by the Holocaust, we're repulsed by race. Determined not to allow any hint of thought that at a distant extreme killed six million Jews, UNESCO sought to abolish mention of race altogether. It preferred ethnic groups. Without race, there's no racism, but if there were really no races, there'd be no genocide. We just like the word.

Combating racism is still the West's primary educational, scientific, and cultural objective. In 2005, the Race, Ethnicity, and Genetics Working Group of the National Human Genome Research Institute made no secret of its starting point. "*The belief that racial and ethnic groups have substantial, well-demarcated biological differences and that these differences are important has contributed to many of the great atrocities of the 20th century and continues to shape personal interactions and social institutions.*"

Other than the Holocaust and Japanese war machine (although we've long lost interest in Japanese racism), I don't know what atrocities the Working Group had in mind. Doctrines of racial and other equality (not superiority) underpinned the far more numerous communist atrocities.

The Working Group criticised race, ethnicity, and ancestry as means of categorising people. Scared to death of where loose talk might lead, we fear the forces that words set forth.

In reviewing the section about shopping in my book that became *Western Individualism*, I wanted to use a word to mean race. The Microsoft word-processing software listed several synonyms for race, but they all related to a contest: competition, battle, chase, pursuit, event, compete, and take part. Synonyms for ethnicity were civilisation, society, mores, traditions, customs, way of life, and background. None of them spoke to biology.

Ethnicity didn't bother Australian zoologist and former television presenter Rob Morrison in 2011. "*Ethnicity,' 'nationality' and 'culture' are useful words in discussions like these*," he wrote, citing UNESCO in his continuing efforts to combat racism, "*because they have a more or less generally accepted meaning, but isn't it time we dropped 'race'?*"

I was surprised to read of ethnicity, nationality, and culture having generally accepted meanings. Through my time in Normandy in 1986, Normans saw themselves quite distinct from the Franks. Whether the English, British, or Europeans are a race is the same question whether they're ethnicities. Whether each is a nationality is just as problematic. Tribes of Australian Aborigines and American Indians call themselves nations, as we call them nations. Few words are more ambiguous in our postmodern West than culture, without biology to assist. None of those words bother us the way race does.

Ethnicity doesn't fare much better than race. When I hear or read of ethnicity, it normally means what we used to call race. Most of us aren't able to mention it, except in the friendliest of fashions at an ethnic communities' council.

Like so many others, Morrison rationalised our condemnation of racism. Also like others, he did so by attacking Europeans. "*Race is an old concept*," he wrote, "*and one greatly bolstered in its time by Europeans' assumptions of superiority over the inhabitants of the countries that they were colonising.*"

"*Physical variations in the human species have no meaning except the social ones that humans put on them*," commented Warren in response. "*The term "race" is a 18th century invention used to rationalise (& maintain) the social inequalities between different groups of people… I would suggest learning some history but I fear it would be a waste of time.*"

Not only do we use notions of science to advance our social policy objectives, we assume our forebears did too. We think they constructed biological distinctions between people to divide and oppress, because (since the Holocaust) we think they did everything to oppress.

Morrison and Warren were doubtlessly sincere, victims of the falsification of history into a story of white people's wickedness, without thinking it through. There's something nonsensical about saying any race or group of races invented the concept of race, as if there'd be no races otherwise: racism without race. All Europeans did was apply a sense of science to people, much as we applied science to everything else. All the peoples of the world understood race to some degree, even if only in the most obviously observable differences. Tribes barely able to do more than drag sticks in the sand distinguished different races as soon as they confronted another, whatever words they happened to use.

Race had been referred to for centuries as we might speak of nations, before our increasingly sophisticated sciences in the seventeenth century focused upon physical and psychological differences and similarities between peoples. Through the ensuing centuries, we led the way in understanding race because we led the way in rational thought. We tried to understand things, through an age of inquiry unlike any in my lifetime, so far.

Our first objective with science was knowledge. I've seen no evidence our objective was to maintain social differences. Nineteenth-century Englishman Charles Dickens wrote novels trying to dispel social inequalities between Europeans. We've lost interest in those inequalities.

Britain abolished the slave trade way back in 1807. She abolished slavery altogether in 1833. That was all long before Charles Darwin published *On the Origin of Species* in 1859. Far from justifying our imagined oppression of others, Darwin's theories of natural selection were at odds with what most people at the time knew to be true. If anything, our sense of other races being inferior led us not to oppress them but to feel a burden to help those less able to help themselves.

No less than others of his era and in spite of his interpretation of history in terms of class and production, the great advocate for the oppressed and founder of communism Karl Marx recognised that races differ in their abilities and capacities to contribute to civilisation. Arguably, race underlay the economic classes upon which Marx focussed.

Marx might have imagined overcoming the biological differences of race, but biological differences they were. Among the many races Marx and his Prussian collaborator Friedrich Engels disparaged were Jews, of whom Marx was one.

Those who think that powerful white people of the past invented race to oppress other races have it back to front.

Increasingly since World War II, powerful people have insisted race isn't real to coax white people out of our racism. Race wasn't a political or social construct. The end of race is.

The Holocaust is never far away. Morrison's article arguing for the abolition of race cited white American, South African, and Nazi German racism. He lumped together *"holocaust deniers, apartheid supporters, religious bigots, opponents of immigration, those who dislike a particular skin colour and more."*

Put another way, the more consumed we are by the Holocaust, then the more vehemently we opposed racial segregation in South Africa and the more we embrace Muslims, want immigration, and like other races. That's certainly true, but only for the West. We don't have the option of accepting the historical reality of the Holocaust while wanting to curtail interracial immigration, for example.

Ours are uniquely Western moralities post Holocaust; we confuse morality with reality. We rejected racism not on scientific grounds but emotional ones, forged in the flames of Holocaust.

Europeans and Jews become two shades of the multitudes. Since the Holocaust, we think that's worthwhile. We reject reality in other contexts as being subjective, but postmodern relativism doesn't apply to matters of race; all our talk about each person's reality falls away. There's no room for different perspectives, no multitude of truths. We think not with faith but conviction, more resolute than belief merely in God. While we might argue to and fro about Deity, there's no argument about race.

Words like Negro and Mongoloid became offensive for reflecting a biological basis for race, although we make exemptions in cases like the United Negro College Fund, founded in 1944, for historical reasons. After all, they help Negroes, who don't mind the name. Only among white people is race an old concept and even then, only sometimes.

The deep trauma of the Holocaust wasn't its brutality, but its civility. These were no barbarous Turks massacring Armenians where they found them, but the most civilised of peoples from the most civilised races on earth, ours, organising victims onto trains to their deaths. It was society and structure, and we lost our last faith in each of them.

We lost the distinction between good and bad societies, but *Obersturmbannführer* Bruno Müller recognised the distinction. He led a unit that killed a hundred and fifty-five Jews in the city of Bender, Moldova in 1941, but only trusted the men who'd burnt "the bridges to respectable society" by murdering someone. When the West took up culpability for the Holocaust, we all burnt those bridges.

We're not fussed about cruelty. When my second son was in year five, his teacher (who was Chinese) gave the class a sheet of paper listing the grounds upon which children shouldn't bully each other, including their skin colour, race, and homosexuality. That evening, my son told me the class was left with the impression that bullying was fine, but not for the reasons listed.

Opposing racism instead of hatred, greed, and other immorality means we replace one motivation with another. People who condone violence bash and murder for brand-named sport shoes. People who condemn violence don't. For the sake of a soccer game and one bad decision, South Americans murder a referee. Hating each other and ourselves became acceptable, although a person bludgeoned near death cares less about the attacker's motivations than the fact of being attacked. I'd rather a person hated me and didn't touch me at all, than was altogether indifferent to me but thrust a knife through my chest for the sake of my wallet.

We equate racism with the Holocaust, but the problem with racial conflict isn't the racism but the conflict. The problem with genocide is the homicide, not the racism. We tarnish racism with the brush of war, but there have been many, many other atrocities. If we reject racism for the millions of deaths at the hands of Nazism, we should reject equality for the tens of millions dead at the hands of socialism. The Holocaust was no more the logical consequence of racism than the many communist massacres were the logical consequence of sharing lunch with a friend. They both required a willingness to kill, with little or no compunction.

People kill and make war if they find killing and war acceptable, acting for all manner of reasons: to keep whatever they value or to get more. Iraqis had long envied Kuwait's vast oil reserves while Kuwaitis partied in the nightclubs of London, when Iraq invaded the rich emirate in 1990. While America and her allies prepared for war not to save us but to repel Iraq, restoring not our countries but Kuwait, I suggested to my colleagues at work that we print captions on tee shirts not quite as polite as "*I couldn't give a damn about Kuwait, but I really like oil."*

Instead of being a call to war, the end of our racism was supposed to end war. It didn't; war doesn't need race. Ending white racism just added more reasons to fight.

Nazism is the political philosophy we fight as if it can never be eradicated, but there have been other philosophies to fight. Senses of ideological superiority killed more people than feelings of racial superiority ever had.

Our causes of killing had been ideological across the crumbling Russian Empire through the end of World War I and across Europe thereafter. In defence of communism from reform or challenge, the Soviet Union invaded Hungary in 1956, Czechoslovakia in 1968, and Afghanistan in 1979. Communists murdered fellow Germans trying to escape East Germany. There's still killing and pillage, but not racist killing and pillage.

Communist North Korea invaded South Korea in 1950. My father told me communists denied the North was the aggressor until its claims of reaching so far into the South made their denials preposterous.

South Vietnamese revolutionaries and North Vietnamese invaders also wanted national reunification under communism. They waged the Vietnam War from 1955.

Since World War II, Western governments have sent their men to fight and die not for our countries and races but to defend other countries and races. Americans in the Korean War included conscripts, but by the time America and Australia sent conscripts to the Vietnam War, a generation convinced white racism was our foe wasn't concerned about communism. It defended Vietnam from us.

Western opponents of communism proved as ideological as the communists, willing to give up our races and countries. Journalist Greg Sheridan told a dinner I attended in 2015 that Australia's most effective force against communism and a devout Roman Catholic, his friend Bob Santamaria, pressed the Australian government to accept Vietnamese refugees after the fall of Saigon in 1975, believing they too opposed communism.

Espousing ideologies of pacifism doesn't make someone peaceful. Early in the 1970s, physician Stuart Wynter was a leader of the movement opposed to Australia's involvement in the Vietnam War, but he was no pacifist at home in Gloucester, north of Newcastle. He pushed his wife Helen Cummings through cupboards, yanked her hair, held her to the floor, chased her with a fishing knife, and smashed furniture and her guitar. "It was like being in a war zone," Cummings said later, "only in a war zone there are mates to share the experience."

She took their two children and left him in 1976, but he married again. Eight years after his first wife left, Wynter murdered his second wife Rakentati and their four-year-old daughter Binatia, before killing himself.

2. EUGENICS

Before being corrupted by ideology and political objectives, science was a pursuit of the truth. The scientific method involves observing the natural or unnatural world and drawing theories from those observations. The theories ought to be logically plausible, or at least not completely ludicrous, however improbable or even shocking they are. If they're logically plausible, then ideally we test them. We perform experiments whenever possible and desirable.

Charles Darwin's 1859 book *On the Origin of Species* inspired his cousin Sir Francis Galton, in his 1883 book *Inquiries into Human Faculty and its Development*, to compose the word "*eugenics.*" It is the science of people by their inherited characteristics. The honorary vice president of the First International Congress of Eugenics in 1912 was Britain's future bulwark against Nazism, Winston Churchill. Other prominent supporters of the congress included Alexander Graham Bell, the inventor of the telephone. Across the scientific world, race was an aspect of eugenics.

Treating Jewish and other prisoners like laboratory rats, physician Josef Mengele performed crude medical experiments at the Auschwitz-Birkenau concentration camp. We've come to presume that Nazi experimentation was all about racial superiority. It wasn't. Most haunting were Mengele's experiments into heredity and disease upon twins. By his callous actions pursuing knowledge indifferent to the suffering involved, Mengele didn't just torture and kill. The pursuit of knowledge that hitherto brought us greatness fell into disrepute, at least about human biology.

We decided knowledge is inseparable from the use of that knowledge: its consequences. Instead of garnering knowledge of heredity with conscience, we gave up on knowledge. We can't exploit knowledge for evil if we don't have knowledge to start with, so we shut down our sense of inquiry; knowledge be damned. In our desire to be everything that science at Auschwitz-Birkenau wasn't, we ended the talk upon which people like Mengele acted.

The pursuit of knowledge wasn't all bad. In 1940, Nazi German scientists were the first to link smoking tobacco with cancer. Several decades would pass before the Western public realised the same thing, while tobacco company executives kept their knowledge to themselves.

What remains in the West are family histories and studies of family we call genealogy, without dwelling upon inherited characteristics. When we rejected racism, we rejected eugenics, although eugenics centred upon creating people rather than killing them. Eugenics was about marriage, babies, and bettering human beings, which in some cases meant sterilising people we thought carried genetic deformities.

Without eugenics, we're still sterilising people, but for other reasons. In 2012, the Washoe County social services department in Nevada petitioned the County Court to abort the eleven-week foetus of mentally retarded and physically disabled Elisa Bauer. The department also wanted Bauer, thirty-two years old, sterilised.

In 2013, Justice Eleanor King in the English Court of Protection approved the sterilisation of a man referred to as D.E., thirty-six years old, believing it to be in his best interests. With a mental age between six and nine years old, he didn't want another child but was incapable of deciding to use contraception.

From eugenics came genes, the more we understood the biological nature of people and our inherited characteristics. In Australia, human genes can be patented.

A 2006 Dutch survey of fourteen thousand seven-year-old twins and more than eight thousand ten-year-old twins concluded that genes account for seventy percent of gender-atypical behaviour in both genders. Genes might affect specific behaviours, desires to associate with the other gender, the rejection of limits, or something else altogether.

I don't understand it, but scientists at Oregon State University reported in 2011 that GG, AG, or AA genotypes for the rs53576 deoxyribonucleic acid (D.N.A.) sequence of the oxytocin receptor gene affect people's kindness and caring. People with two copies of the G allele are more empathetic, trusting, and loving. Those with AG or AA genotypes feel less positive overall and less parental sensitivity. They might also have a higher risk of autism. "Our findings suggest even slight genetic variation may have tangible impact on people's behaviour," said lead author Aleksandr Kogan, a psychology researcher at the University of Toronto, "and that these behavioural differences are quickly noticed by others."

"It may not be that we need to fix people who exhibit less social traits," said senior author Sarina Rodrigues Saturn, a psychology professor at Oregon State University, "but that we recognise they are overcoming a genetically influenced trait, and that they may need more understanding and encouragement." Her earlier research established a genetic role in empathy.

In 2012, biological psychologist Christian Montag from the University of Bonn reported genetic links in women being obsessed with social networking and retail websites. He and colleagues had interviewed more than eight hundred people inquiring into their computer habits, thoughts, and feelings about losing computer network access. They then looked at the genetic composition of one hundred and thirty-two people who seemed most addicted to the network, comparing them to a healthy control group. Many of the hundred and thirty-two had the same genetic variant, which had previously been linked to nicotine addiction. "The current data already shows that there are clear indications for genetic causes of internet addiction," said Montag.

In 2013, the Productivity Commission report *Deep and Persistent Disadvantage in Australia* included parents' cognitive abilities and inherited genes among the five causes of differences in academic performance between children from the richest and poorest families. It cited a British study suggesting inherited cognitive abilities explain one-fifth of the difference, after adjusting for environmental factors.

We retain a touch of eugenics when we screen sperm donors for genetic diseases, although Danish health officials in 2012 reported a Danish sperm donor having passed the genetic nerve disorder Neurofibromatosis type I, sometimes known as Von Recklinghausen's disease, to five children after a screening test at the Copenhagen clinic Nordisk Cryobank failed to identify the disease in him. Symptoms of Von Recklinghausen's disease can include beige patches on the skin, high blood pressure, bone deformity, scoliosis, learning difficulties, and eye problems including tumours on the optic nerve. The donor reportedly fathered forty-three children at fourteen clinics.

Other races aren't as reticent as we are about eugenics. China passed its Law on Maternal and Infant Health Care in 1994, becoming effective in 1995. Article 10 prevents people with serious genetic diseases from marrying, unless they take measures not to fall pregnant. Article 16 obliges married couples of childbearing age with serious genetic diseases to take similar measures.

Evolutionary psychologist Geoffrey Miller wrote *The Mating Mind: How Sexual Choice Shaped the Evolution of Human Nature* in 2001. In 2013, he wrote that the *"most likely result"* of Chinese eugenics programmes *"is that America and Europe linger around a few hundred more years as also-rans on the world historical stage, nursing our anti-hereditarian political correctness to the bitter end."*

We're not reticent about applying eugenics to crops, plants, and animals. In 2013, computational biologist Peter Ralph thought the genes of a particular kind of tree might reveal something about how that species responded to glaciation. He also contemplated analysing the genes of humpback whales to learn about population sizes before whaling.

Our determination not to reinforce racial stereotypes stymied genetic research into diseases more prevalent among indigenous peoples, although things were changing by 2012. "What we've seen in the past couple of years is that tide of opinion start to reverse," said anthropologist Emma Kowal from Melbourne University's School of Social and Political Sciences, before the release of research into diabetes and middle ear infections among Aborigines. It was the first research in nearly a decade investigating genetic causes of disease in Aborigines.

Also under way were studies into genetic associations with heart disease, kidney disease, and vulval cancer among Aborigines. The human papilloma virus causing cervical cancer occurred in Arnhem Land women at seventy times the national Australian rate.

Through the preceding two years, Australians had been developing specific guidelines for collecting, storing, and using Aboriginal biological specimens like those already developed in Canada for her indigenous peoples. "We may see more research, we may see less," said Kowal, "but we definitely will see indigenous communities better equipped to engage with genetic researchers and to decide whether they want to pursue genetic research projects." Researchers would explain genetic concepts to Aboriginal communities.

Our fear of genetic research is our fear of another Holocaust. Common among East European Jews, the three Ashkenazi Jewish genetic mutations briefly became infamous in 2013 when actress Angelina Jolie underwent surgery to remove her breasts because she carried one of them. Two mutations on the BRCA1 gene raise the risk of breast cancer by seventy percent. One on the BRCA2 gene raises the risk by fifty percent. The gene also increases the risk of developing ovarian cancer by dozens of percentage points.

Head of the Department of Medical Genetics at Shaare Zedek Hospital in Israel, geneticist Efrat Levi-Lahad examined eight thousand healthy Ashkenazi men in 2012. One hundred and seventy-five of them carried an Ashkenazi mutation. Among female relatives of the carriers, the risk of developing breast or ovarian cancer was between seventy-five and eighty percent. Researchers recommended a policy of general genetic testing for the presence of the mutations among the entire Ashkenazi population in Israel.

Anthropologists speaking at the 2014 annual American Association for the Advancement of Science conference in Chicago complained about genetic sequencing and other scientific research spreading the belief that races exist and differ as regards biology, behaviour, and culture. Calling it "neoracism" (although I'm not sure why it isn't just racism), they were particularly concerned about published research showing, for example, that Africans are more likely than European peoples to carry the blood type causing sickle cell disease and protecting people against malaria.

We want individualism. "Genome science can help us a lot in the individualisation of medical practice," said Nina Jablonski, an anthropologist at Pennsylvania State University, while warning that science could be "misused" to propagate the belief that people inherently have different abilities because of their race.

"Compared with animals, in which race effectively means subspecies, humans prove remarkably similar, with genetic variations occurring largely within supposed racial groups rather than across them," wrote Rob Morrison in his 2011 article arguing for the abolition of race. He placed great credence in the United Nations Educational, Scientific, and Cultural Organisation in 1950 insisting *"that science had shown humans to be a species, that cultural rather than genetic factors accounted for much of the observed variation between them, and that the "layperson use of the term 'race'" should be dropped altogether in favour of "ethnic groups." That was more than 60 years ago, and DNA studies make it look pretty prescient now."*

Science had shown no such thing, except to us determined post-Holocaust to see only similarities between people and put aside differences. Where there are genes, there used to be race.

The eldest of my young children and I were among a minority of white people in the audience attending a talk about human evolution at the Seventh Day Adventist church in Waitara early in the new millennium. The people addressing us were, as I recall, also Western. One speaker said the genetic differences between races were only about one percent of the genes in human beings, which he claimed made racism irrational. The audience applauded; nothing is surer to elicit applause from an audience in a Western country, whatever the audience's racial composition, than a reason to reject racism. Nothing warms white people more than applause from other races.

The speaker omitted to mention (or mightn't have known) that by such a measure, genetic differences between human beings and chimpanzees are less than two percent. We can't dismiss a difference of one percent of our genes without dismissing two percent almost as readily. There are thirty thousand or so genes in human beings.

It hardly matters that the percentage of genetic differences between races could be much more than one percent, depending upon our definitions. Noah Rosenberg from the University of Southern California, Los Angeles and six other researchers published a report in *Science* magazine in 2002 analysing the variations in three hundred and seventy-seven genotypes from a thousand and fifty-six people among fifty-two populations around the world. They concluded that differences between individuals within a population account for ninety-three to ninety-five percent of genetic variation and that differences between major groups (what we might call races) constitute from three to five percent. They identified six main genetic clusters, five of which correspond to major geographic regions, and sub-clusters often corresponding to particular populations. The genetic differences between sub-clusters within a continent, such as Swedes in Europe and the Hmong in Asia, are about fifteen percent.

Rather than interpreting the results as affirmation that races are biologically real, Larry Adelman, executive producer of the television documentary *Race: The Power of an Illusion*, rejected race as genetic reality because genetic variations are greater within races than between them. It was essentially the same argument employed by Morrison and by the Race, Ethnicity, and Genetics Working Group of the National Human Genome Research Institute in a 2005 article, 'The use of racial, ethnic and ancestral categories in human genetics research.' Indeed, it's the only supposedly scientific rationale I've seen advanced for our rejection of race: the range of behaviours, features, and traits within races often exceeds the differences between races.

It's a rejection of statistical variances, asserting, for example, that one race being on average taller than another is immaterial because some individuals are taller than others by a greater extent. It's more than saying Zulus are the same as Pygmies because we find a tall Pygmy taller than a short Zulu. It's enough if the difference between the average heights of Zulus and Pygmies is less than the range of heights among Zulus or among Pygmies, even if the shortest of Zulus is still taller than the tallest of Pygmies.

"But just because some members of a population might carry a specific gene form," wrote Adelman, *"doesn't mean all members do."* We reject biological race because we reject biological generalisation, although we don't apply such a strict rationale to matters other than race. We don't reject a link between smoking tobacco and lung cancer because a smoker doesn't contract cancer and a non-smoker does. We don't suggest climatic seasons aren't real because some days in winter are warmer than some days in summer, or because the range of temperatures within summer and winter is greater than the difference between their averages.

Our rejection of race is Western individualism. Anything less than a one hundred percent genetic difference between races means we reject race as a biological concept, but we're also rejecting race where there's a hundred percent difference between races. It's abundantly clear some physical traits occur throughout races.

Pointing to the failure of multiracialism, Africans in America have among the highest rates of hypertension in the world. West Africans in Africa have among the lowest. Adelman blamed the former, at least in part, upon living in racist America. Adelman thus recognised a racial reality, placing race in the context of society. *"Race may be a biological myth,"* he claimed, *"a social construction, but it nonetheless remains very real. It can even have biological effects."*

In our social construction, race is real because racism is. We think we eliminate race by eliminating racism. We don't.

3. SELECTIVE GENETICS

When our sciences sought knowledge, we categorised varieties of fauna and flora into species, subspecies, and genus, without anyone suggesting that was to oppress celery. The Botanic Gardens in Melbourne in December 2012 included a small blue plaque headed *"Strength in Diversity,"* but they weren't just different species of plants. They were different species of camellias: more than two hundred and seventy of them. *"They mostly originate from China, but also Japan, Vietnam and other parts of Asia."*

While we continue to dwell upon the differences between plants to denote each of them a species, we've discarded the differences between races of people to deem human beings a species and never anything less. *"What does racism mean if there are no human races and if the human race is actually a species?"* asked Rob Morrison in 2011, as I've never read anyone asking of camellias.

Species of cats, dogs, and anything else are much like races of people. We have as much reason to respect or discard the differences between beagles and poodles as we do between races of people.

If there's confusion in language then the phrase "human race" created it. We could speak of a human species, whereby races are subspecies within it. Applying the same semantics as flora and fauna, we'd speak of races and ethnicities as species and subspecies. In the end, it's a matter of nomenclature, but if human beings are a species, then so are camellias. So is a kitten by the side of the porch and a lion preparing to kill, however unlikely they are to mate.

When we're investigating genes early in the twenty-first century, we set careful limits to avoid promoting racism. We have no limits looking for reasons to reject racism. In its 2005 article 'The use of racial, ethnic and ancestral categories in human genetics research,' the Race, Ethnicity, and Genetics Working Group of the National Human Genome Research Institute called upon scientists to *"demonstrate the irrelevance of racial and ethnic labels"* by *"emphasising the close genetic affinities between members of different groups."* It's selective genetics.

In 2013, computational biologist Peter Ralph and geneticist Graham Coop reported their analyses of half a million locations on the genome (encoded in deoxyribonucleic acid, D.N.A.) known to vary from person to person, along with language and country of origin information, among more than two thousand people living in forty countries across Europe and Turkey. People with common sequences in their genome had common ancestors, with the longer the common sequence the more recent their common ancestor. The shortest common sequences suggested a common ancestor as much as a hundred generations or three thousand years ago.

Ralph and Coop found people living closer together were generally (with several exceptions) more closely related than those living further apart, although their analysis of south-eastern Europe simply picked up the consequences of invasions of Huns and Slavs after the fall of the Roman Empire. More interestingly, people in Britain generally shared one such sequence with each other but were slightly less than twenty percent likely to share one with someone in Turkey. There are three billion base pairs in each genome.

Whether the people living in Britain who shared a common sequence with someone in Turkey were racially British or resident in Britain but of another race wasn't clear from the report. Given that Turks themselves were invaders from Asia, these might have been relations by rape.

The more races appear biologically real, the more we insist that they're not. University of Chicago geneticist John Novembre focused upon the incidences of commonality between a British resident and a Turk, although those with common genome sequences amounted to less than twenty percent of the sample. He ignored the more than eighty percent of pairs of people without common sequences.

Novembre also extrapolated the results to the rest of the earth. "It's a nice illustration of how interconnected human ancestry is," he commented. "It's been expected theoretically, but here they show it empirically."

The *Los Angeles Times* newspaper enthusiastically reported that everyone on earth is related, "*Going back a few thousand years…*"

We in the West feel no affinity with our great-grandparents born less than a century before us, or even our grandparents or parents still with us, but we grab any chance to feel related to other races because of a chance less than one in five we share ancestors who died three thousand years ago. We don't identify with our first and second cousins born of our race, but with people who might possibly be our hundredth cousins because they're not of our race.

John Hawks, a paleoanthropologist at the University of Wisconsin in Madison, pointed out that many "key insights" about humanity's past remained hidden in the human genome. "Europe happens to have a really good genetic sample and really good match of geography to genetic variation," he said. "In some other parts of the world, like Africa, things are not so simple."

We interpret genes to dismiss races. Other races interpret genes to define them. While we hone in upon particular genes to imagine everyone being related to each other, other races hone in upon genes proving we're not.

In the West, we have neither national identities nor debate, but the growing Muslim population in Lebanon has led to debate there about national identity. Christian Maronites claim ancestry from the Phoenicians: intrepid seafarers and tradesmen credited by many (although not by Arabs) with creating the first widely used alphabet, reducing sounds of speech into symbols. More than three thousand years after they sailed the Mediterranean Sea and settled in Lebanon isn't enough time for them to share a common identity with Arabs, said historian Boutros Labaki in 2010. "The decades-old debate over how you define yourself as a Lebanese persists."

When asked to define her identity, Lebanese student Rebecca Yazbeck replied, "I am a Phoenician, not an Arab." Her hair was blonde and eyes were green. "I don't think the Lebanese are Arabs. Civilisations have evolved, but we have been here for centuries." Thirty or so, in fact.

Phoenicians are defined by their race, not their locale, however many millennia they've lived in Lebanon. Pierre Zalloua, a Lebanese scientist whose research tracing the genetic origin of Middle Eastern peoples was published in the *American Journal of Human Genetics and Annals of Human Genetics*, found thirty percent of Lebanese carried what he called "*Phoenician genes*," including some Muslims.

Most races are advantaged by greater populations, but not American Indians. Their tribe is more than a matter of identity. It's a matter of money.

While we imagine wealth reducing racism and other biological tribalism, American Indian wealth since they began operating casinos on their reservations in the 1980s accentuated it. Not so keen to share their riches with others as we are, Indian tribes cast off people not of their tribe. Tribes cancelled their tribal citizenship, financial entitlements, right to vote in tribal elections, and children's access to tribal schools.

Cherokee Indians expelled two thousand eight hundred Africans, known as Freedmen. Two centuries earlier, Cherokees who owned Southern plantations also owned Negro slaves, which many Cherokee took with them when they moved to what became Oklahoma. The Cherokee fought with the South in the Civil War, after which, in 1866, they signed a treaty with the American government awarding the freed slaves tribal citizenship irrespective of whether the freed slaves carried Cherokee blood.

Reading their history, I learnt slave owners and secessionists in America weren't only white. More interesting still was what happened a century and a half later. In 2011, the Cherokee Supreme Court supported the tribe's right to change its constitution on citizenship matters. A new definition of citizen excluded the Freedmen who couldn't prove they had Cherokee blood relations. This was a biological definition completely unconcerned with anything cultural. Race and tribe were no social construct.

Indian tribes expelled Africans. They also expelled mixed-tribe Indians whose forebears identified with other tribes.

"It's like I'm now a white girl with Okie kids," lamented Nikah Dondero, a mother of two. Her mother was evicted from the Picayune Rancheria of the Chukchansi Indians because her great-grandfather, Jack Roan, who died in 1942, declared himself to be a member of another tribe in his will and personal affidavits. An enrolment committee appointed by the Tribal Council rejected evidence to the contrary for having been prepared by white people, such as census information and a photograph by Edward Curtis who'd called Roan a Chukchansi in a photograph in the 1920s.

Tribal governments paid companies to examine people's genes. They retained lawyers and researchers to examine government archives. The Chukchansi hired a former official from the Bureau of Indian Affairs to review every member's bloodline. In the decade to the end of 2011, at least two dozen tribes in California evicted at least two and a half thousand Indians (of more than three hundred and sixty thousand Indians in California) not of their tribal bloodlines.

"The tribe has historically had the ability to remove people," explained Kevin Bearquiver, deputy director for the Pacific region at the Bureau of Indian Affairs. "Tolerance is a European thing brought to the country. We never tolerated things. We turned our back on people." (It was a more positive view of European colonisation and its impact on American Indians than anything else I'd heard in recent years.)

Australian Aborigines were the same. I was told by David (the president of the parents and citizens association at my eldest son's high school) that Aboriginal parents fearing violence from other Aborigines abandoned not only mixed-race babies but also babies born of fathers from other tribes. They were some of the neglected Aboriginal children that Australian governments placed with white foster parents until the 1970s, for which white Australia would later apologise.

We turn our backs on ourselves. We find biological relationships painful.

Genes were at the fore when Belgian customs official Marc Vermeeren and journalist Jean-Paul Mulders found three great-grandchildren of Adolf Hitler's father, Alois, living in Long Island, New York in 2009. The three had fled Germany to escape the Nazis but, sixty-four years after Hitler and his bride committed suicide and the Second World War ended, Vermeeren and Mulders spied on the three for seven days and nights. As if they were monitoring a killer instead of a sixty-year-old retired psychologist who helped Vietnam War veterans, Vermeeren and Mulders watched Alexander eating fried chicken in a fast-food restaurant. When he threw his paper serviette into a bin, they took the serviette. They matched his deoxyribonucleic acid to Hitler.

Vermeeren and Mulders believed thirty-nine relatives of Hitler were alive in 2009. They'd spent an inordinate amount of time looking into it, while other mass murderers hadn't had their family trees studied so closely. Arab terrorist leader Osama bin Laden's huge family was monitored, but we afforded his relatives the benefit of individual innocence. American-born Wafah Dufour was a glamorous model and singer.

Individualism doesn't excuse white people from guilt. Two

other relatives of Hitler living in New York were Louis and Brian Stuart-Houston, residing in a little wooden house in East Patchogue and working as gardeners. "The American relatives have agreed not to have children to extinguish the saga of Hitler," said Mulders of the three, "and stop living in fear."

If theirs was familial guilt, then it was steeped in biology. If they feared those children never born were going to be like Hitler, they ignored any role of individual choice or environmental factors upon human behaviour. It was eugenics, but our pre-war eugenicists never went so far as to reject all other factors and influences: nature and nurture contribute to a person's character.

Those genetic tests provided evidence of Hitler's paternal grandfather (or another close relative of Hitler's father) being Jewish. Saliva taken from the thirty-nine relatives revealed the family carried the chromosome Haplogroup E1b1b1, which is rare in Western Europe but most common among the Berbers of Morocco, Algeria, and Tunisia and among Ashkenazi and Sephardic Jews. It's a major founding lineage of the Jewish population, appearing in approximately eighteen to twenty percent of Y-chromosomes in Ashkenazi Jews and from eight to thirty percent in Sephardic Jews. "*One can from this postulate that Hitler was related to people whom he despised*," wrote Mulders in the Belgian magazine *Knack* in 2010.

Large numbers of Germans and other European peoples feel as Hitler's relatives felt. We do so as a race.

So convicted have we become of our biological guilt, we envisage our children being evil embryos. In 2009, Doc Morris Pharmacies advertised condoms with Hitler, bin Laden, and Chinese dictator Mao Zedong as human sperm. The risk our children could become like those men were reason for us not to become parents.

No German complained about the Hitler sperm. Arabs knew it wasn't the time to complain about mention of bin Laden, not when public opinion was reason to distance themselves publicly from him. China's official media and several Chinese complained at the advertisement's slight on the long-dead Mao.

Chinese people suffered immensely under Mao, but that's a matter for them. It's not something for us to portray. Advertising agency Grey Worldwide, which made the advertisement, sent a letter of apology to the Chinese consulate in Frankfurt. (A year earlier, French carmaker Peugeot Citroen apologised for an advertisement in Spain that portrayed Mao as a cross-eyed old man.)

So if our people or all people were to fade away, then the world would have fewer wrongdoers. We don't appreciate ourselves enough to imagine the great arts and sciences, music and technologies, that would be lost without us. Portraying Johann Sebastian Bach, Vincent van Gogh, or Victor Hugo as human sperm won't sell condoms. It would also reek of the eugenics we've rejected, but ours remains eugenics nevertheless: self-loathing eugenics.

In reality, the babies we bear won't be the likes of Hitler, Mao, or bin Laden. They might be something like Bach, van Gogh, or Hugo, but won't be them. Most likely, they'll be as ordinary and extraordinary as we are. They'll be the right and wrong: people who could be good, as we wish we were good. Whether we love it or loathe it, they'll be us, sharing our hopes and fears, strengths and failings, as we might share theirs.

We're not so evil. We might be lunatics, but very few of us are bad.

We're people whom our business colleagues and suppliers want to succeed and people our competitors want to overcome. We're people working hard in ambition to do everything we can, and people working hard because we've nothing else to do. We're people proudly doing everything, and people proudly doing nothing. We're people who crave wealth and all things material, reputation, and prestige, and people who detest those cravings we see in others. We're people not trying to be anything, running away from being something else. We're people fearful of what we might lose and people so secure we chase exhilaration risking death in our adventure. "The chance that you might die makes you feel alive!" exhorted one thrill-seeking sportsman about whom I read, shortly before his self-invited death.

4. RACIAL DIFFERENCE

Our postmodern notion that all people are equal owes much to communism, although we're more likely to cite the American Declaration of Independence in 1776. America was founded upon words and ideas drawn from European schools of philosophical thought. Thomas Jefferson's statement that all men are created equal was one of fairness, not science. Americans were declaring themselves equals of the British, but also granting all Europeans in America equal opportunity in a land supposed to be without aristocracy and class.

Jefferson never doubted the reality of race. His notes on the State of Virginia contained insightful analysis of the natural world, intriguing political and social commentary, and several racial stereotypes. Had the Declaration of Independence prohibited Negro slavery, the new political union, America, would not have come into being with the states it did. It wouldn't have grown as it did until 1861.

The trouble with founding countries upon words and ideas is that words change their meanings. Ideas depend upon the people thinking them. We changed the way we thought after the Holocaust.

Our rules of race are complex, requiring us to laud other races without labelling them with characteristics that explain why we laud them. The races that come to the fore when we're espousing diversity quickly evaporate. We don't speak of the features of faces smiling back at us from brightly coloured posters or television screens, but they might be a little something of what we mean when we wear tee shirts emblazoned with our oxymoronic slogans *"The same, but different,"* and *"Different, but the same."* When we're not trying to make everyone the same, we're insisting we already are.

Having decided to see only similarities between people, we insist we're the same, but our rhetoric of sameness contradicts our edicts of diversity; diversity is difference. The differences we don't specify, but we aren't so racist as to consider what they are and whether they matter. We dismiss them for being inconsequential or trivialise them beyond recognition, in spite of us celebrating them. We could similarly reject any difference between baked custard tarts and blueberry ice cream because they both contain milk, or between a cow and a milk truck.

We can't believe people are the same and different, but keep trying to do so. If we're the same, then we're not different. If we're different, then we're not all the same. If we truly believed all people are the same, there'd be no diversity. If we thought races were different but equal, we wouldn't bother celebrating. Really, we can't get that far.

If we pause to think what either of them means, we'd see human sameness and racial difference. If that means anything, it's because we have human nature with racial traits.

We talk of seeing the person instead of the race, but the person is the race, along with other definition. Until the Second World War, we had a wealth of scientific knowledge and theories about race, relating to physical features, intellect, psyche, and even soul; people didn't need to be scientists to recognise different temperaments between races. Today, we laugh at them: at every earnest belief by our forebears that race is real. (We don't laugh at other races; that would be rude.)

We treat race in ways unlike our treatment of anything else, striving to avert racial generalisations with far more fear than we feel for perpetuating other generalisations. In reviewing my non-fiction writing about individualism I then called *Homo Capitalisticus*, a manuscript assessor told me I needed only one example to make my point. Any more was repetitive or, worse still, boring.

When my writing ventured near matters related to race (or gender, for that matter), no end of examples was enough. I was accused of making generalisations.

More than offending people of another race, they offend white people certain that racial forces are never in play. They also play into the minds of people silly enough to think they are.

Fearful of promoting racism among people not as clever as we are, we're careful what we measure, without being confident of the outcome. We study not race but racism.

In 1999, the American Department of Justice and New Jersey attorney general got it wrong. They commissioned the Public Services Research Institute in Maryland to carry out a statistical investigation of speeding drivers to provide evidence that New Jersey state troopers were racist, after twenty-three percent of drivers they'd booked for speeding were black. Instead, examination of photographs of speeding drivers revealed that twenty-five percent of speeders were black. Adjusted for age and gender, blacks were twice as likely as whites to speed. The racial disparity was even greater among drivers travelling at more than ninety miles per hour.

Speeding Blacks were thus less likely to be booked than speeding whites. Rather than rejecting the allegations of racism, New Jersey attorney general David Samson in 2002 rejected the study. He said New Jersey troopers had already admitted they engaged in racial profiling.

Europeans have too many different colours of hair and eyes for them ever to be at the forefront of our thinking. Trying hard not to make racial inquiries, we reduce race to skin colour: black, brown, olive, red, yellow, and white. We still try our darnedest not to notice it. Other races notice.

We think the children of immigrants meld freely into their new populations, but actress Lucy Liu spoke of being a banana (yellow on the outside, white on the inside) while promoting her 2007 film *Code Name: The Cleaner* in an interview with Sheila Roberts. No white person would use such terms in so public a place, but few white people can still imagine such a concept as colour in a brain any more than in skin. "I think when you grow up Asian American," said Liu, "it's difficult because you don't know if you're Asian or you're American. You get confused…"

From a Singaporean Chinese professor addressing alumni at the Macquarie Graduate School of Management some years earlier, I'd first heard the description of East Asians born in the West as bananas. Similarly, South Asians and Africans describe their emigrants in the West as coconuts (brown on the outside, white on the inside). Calling people bananas or coconuts is derisory; acting a little like one race while being another makes people crazy. More than the lunacy of multiracial environments, it's a separation between people acting according to their race and those compromised.

A combination of inherited features and environmental factors shape people and the choices they make. What's true of individuals is true of races.

To initiate its Christmas season, the St Ives Shopping Village convened a fair the third Sunday in November, 2010. The man sixty or so years old operating the plaster fun house was smart enough to know that being conversational was good for business. He talked about the friendly people with whom he dealt, but also about the people always looking for the edge. The Mandarin Centre at Chatswood (affectionately called "Chats-Woo" by my Jewish friend Ian Biner, the day we met for lunch at a Chinese restaurant there) employed him to provide shoppers' children with free plaster painting. Some adults used all manner of excuses, like sitting with their babies, as excuses to get more plaster painting without paying for it. Others returned, insisting they hadn't previously received their free plaster painting. "I know what you Asians are like," he told them. "I know. I married a Chinese girl."

My experiences of Chinese through my corporate career were much the same, but most of us can't cite a foreign spouse to defend ourselves from accusations of racism. My wife worked in a Chinese restaurant when she was a teenage girl. (She was no less a white Australian then.) The Chinese restaurant manager paid her less money and treated her worse than did the McDonalds restaurant at which she also worked, although we complain about American hamburger restaurants allegedly mistreating workers as we'd never complain about Chinese restaurants.

We imagine racial diversity teaching us about other races but then reject racial generalisations, not because our representative samples are too small or because they may not be true in every instant. We refuse to countenance them even if they are true in every instant.

Around about 1990, Australian football coach Ron Barassi remarked that the Footscray Football Club was losing its supporter base because Vietnamese immigrants to inner-city Melbourne weren't interested in Australian football. His words caused an immediate outcry, although he meant no insult. (Some people might say he meant a compliment.) Journalists quickly found a Vietnamese person in the crowd at a football game (or brought him along for the photograph). Suddenly, their dearth among the hundreds of thousands of fans cramming grounds each weekend was immaterial.

As the Footscray club neared collapse, a commentator criticised the club's management for failing to tap into the Vietnamese psyche. Racial differences that supposedly don't exist if they hint at reasons not to welcome immigrants become a reason for criticising white people when we don't adapt to them. The club became the Western Bulldogs, with the mysterious initials "F.F.C." on its jerseys, and moved to the western suburbs of Melbourne.

Two decades later, Lin Jong began playing in the Australian Football League. No other debut player had the attention afforded him from the league's media network that second Sunday in August 2012: our proof positive that all races are the same and everybody watching football should know it. Funnily enough, he played for the Western Bulldogs. It must've tapped into somebody's psyche.

There doesn't need to be anything derogatory in what someone theorises about races for us to object. Even apparently neutral generalisations, such as whether black Americans really eat fried chicken more than other races eat it, all else being equal, speak to something about race.

They can even be compliments, of sorts. Mixed-race golfer Tiger Woods had just been exposed as a serial philanderer when radio personality Kyle Sandilands asked Devon James in 2010, "Because we heard that he's, like, massive, like a donkey, is that right?"

"Yeah, I'd agree," replied James.

Fellow radio personality Jackie O asked James about how Woods ranked as a lover. She too asked after the size of his most masculine anatomy.

There mightn't have been a controversy had the conversation ended there because the questions focused upon one man, but then Sandilands asked, "Were you surprised…, 'Man, you're half Asian, half black, obviously the half black is what's going on downstairs'?" Simply posing the question was controversial.

Anti-Discrimination Board president Stepan Kerkyasharian was appalled. "There is a racial element here," he complained, "there is stereotyping involved." (Kerkyasharian probably didn't laugh very often.) "These remarks are not a joke," he said. "They create an environment which is saying that you can classify people according to their colour and race, and then attach to them various attributes."

There's to be no classification of people by race: no attempts to consider what attributes might attach to particular races. There aren't to be any racial truisms or traits, because there aren't to be races. We've crushed the notion of race.

Ignorance and stupidity are charges we make against white people harbouring any racial thought or feeling, while shutting ourselves away from any risk that they're right. Our refusal to consider whether human beings have something called race, let alone learn what it might mean, isn't just wilful ignorance. It's mandatory ignorance we foist upon each other; a lot of ignorance and presumption brought us to where we are. About matters of race, we can't so much as wonder.

The year after Sandilands' remarks, in 2011, Judge Sulet Potterill of the Pretoria High Court halted a shipment of eleven million female condoms from China for three reasons. One reason was that they were too small. A South African firm, Sekunjalo Investments Corporation, could supply condoms twenty percent larger.

Perhaps with a little nudging, when the facts are overwhelming but unimportant, we might reluctantly admit to there being racial traits. Bravely, we might suggest races are manifest in colours of skin, but dare not think as far as hair colours and textures, eye folds, bone structures, nose shapes, or the distribution of fat across faces, all of which vary between races.

A Japanese character in the 1967 film *You Only Live Twice* asked of British spy James Bond, "You know what it is about you that fascinates them, don't you? It's the hair on your chest. Japanese men all have beautiful bare skin."

Of course, it was only a film, for which a Welshman wrote the screenplay. An Englishman wrote the book, from which the film was loosely derived.

There is a myriad of physical differences between races, but we're not even cautiously racist; our racial blindness is to much more than colour. It obscures from us all manner of facts, but we don't want a cure to alleviate it.

It's not really blindness, but simply closing our eyes and fiercely keeping them closed. Those differences gave rise to race in the first place. They maintain them among other races.

Every feature that varies in frequency or degree between people might also vary between races. The variances between races might be more, less, or the same as those within. They might be statistically significant and still mean nothing at all. If we knew what they were, we could decide to do nothing about them. We could utilise them, or at least take them into account. They might be important.

We refuse information, and would rather not ask questions than risk answers we don't like. We won't consider that race might be more than skin pigments in our forebears' imaginations.

There could be a thousand racial stereotypes soundly grounded in reality or none, but still they're starting points for what more we can study. In our aversion to prejudice, we miss our chance to learn, to better ourselves and others as our nineteenth-century forebears did.

Generalisations have their limitations, but can still be true. Without them, we can't learn. I generalise about white people knowing I'm often referring only to the economically powerful and politically doctrinaire, but they're the ones who speak loudest. They're often the only ones speaking at all. They purport to represent their people and do, but daren't presume to speak for all people through all time. Inescapably together, they share cause for what we're doing now.

We have no quest to know, not about race. We don't even ask; we've already decided. While we might wonder about God and make our inquiry, we don't want to learn about race. We're all-consuming race deniers, determined to deny the existence of race. Proud to do what do, we don't even consider what challenges our convictions about the way people are. We prohibit the possibility of a natural correlation between race and anything else, or between multiracialism and anything bad.

We confuse racially charged wrongs of the past with knowledge about race altogether, but if we could satisfy ourselves there would be no more Jewish Holocausts, at least committed by us, we could again open our minds to consider carefully what facts might be. Speculation can be useful, provided we know we're speculating.

Racism might or might not be rational. Certainly irrational is the West's refusal since the Holocaust even to entertain a suggestion that race could be biologically real, with psychological, mental, and important physical differences between races. Our fears of race and white racism are so plainly irrational, our mental illness is racophobia. Indifferent or oblivious to reality, we're at war against knowledge.

5. INSTITUTIONAL WHITE RACISM

Having rejected inherited characteristics between people, we reject biological differences between people. Thus we are unwaveringly resolute that all people are the same: that all races left free will perform equally.

We insist people are the same in spite of any number of differences, but those differences between countries, cultures, values, and behaviours are reasons to wonder whether there might be differences between races. Bangkok is clearly not Berlin, Apia so different from Athens. If we contrast arts and crafts, the differences might be even more.

Rejecting biological components to human values and behaviour, we attribute differences between countries and races to something other than race, such as political systems, material wealth, and weather. We thus conclude that all races in the same environment (such as a city or school) should be the same, although Japan and Iceland are much the same environments. Japanese are still different to Icelanders.

We assume equality is justice, as if the universe is innately fair. Thus difference becomes injustice.

In our vision of people post Holocaust, differences between races don't cause racism. Racism causes racial differences.

Institutional white racism can be any law, structure, programme, or anything else by which races remain unequal in the West. The only evidence it exists are the disparities between races, but those disparities are unmistakeable. Certain as we are that races aren't real, or that all races are equal, our last explanation for particular races remaining disproportionately poor, unemployed, imprisoned, uneducated, incompetent, or unhealthy is white people's racism of some form or another. The lack of other evidence of our racism isn't a problem. It simply proves how extensive and intrinsic our inadvertent racism must be.

Ours is a neat, self-fulfilling circle of logic. Racial disparities are evidence of institutional white racism. Institutional white racism explains racial disparities. Having eliminated overt white racism and without any sense of biological or other superiority, it's the subliminal racism white people don't intend but must have anyway. Black American Imani Perry, professor at the Centre for African American Studies at Princeton University, wrote of post-intentional white racism in her 2011 book *More Beautiful and More Terrible: The Embrace and Transcendence of Racial Inequality in the United States.* It's our failure to overcome race.

We can't be satisfied we've eradicated racism until rates of everything are the same across races: we're identical. Seized by the reality of race, racial equality presupposes race.

By 2012, half the students at Harvey Scott School in Portland, Oregon were Hispanic and another fifteen percent black. Verenice Gutierrez, the school principal, blamed their poor academic results upon the minority of white American students mentioning lunch. She thought it made other races, even the more numerous Hispanics, feel excluded. "What about Somali or Hispanic students, who might not eat sandwiches?" she asked. "Another way would be to say: 'Americans eat peanut butter and jelly, do you have anything like that?' Let them tell you. Maybe they eat torta, or pita."

The Portland School District wasn't focused on education but racial equity. We equate equity to equality, certain that any apparent inequality can't be due to real inequality. We don't just think races are equal in every conceivable way. We want them to be.

Implementing the language of 'Courageous Conversations,' meant white educators understanding their supposed racial privilege. They had to change their teaching practices to improve academic results among other races.

Most, if not all, Portland's school principals had been through Glenn Singleton's 'Coaching for Educational Equity,' a week-long seminar on race and its effects on life. (I suspect race as a biological reality never came up, except to reject it.) The district's administrative committee met every second week not to discuss race but to address systematic white racism.

Asians and Jews outperform Somalis and Hispanics at school, but we don't imagine talk of sandwiches affecting their academic results. (We credit their success, but not ours, to intellect and hard work.) We don't think so much about the successes and failings of other races relative to each other but only to us, when they're faring worse than we are. So do they. "That's your white privilege," insisted Gutierrez, defending special lunchtime drum classes for black and Latino boys at Harvey Scott, Vernon, and Faubion schools, "and your whiteness."

Race remains. By 2015, America's Department of Education demanded to know the proportion of black, Latino, and white students (but apparently not Asians or Jews) enrolled in advanced placement classes and those for gifted and talented students in all public schools across the country. The department's Civil Rights Office stood ready to investigate and prosecute any schools where blacks and Latinos were under-enrolled in those classes to a "statistically significant degree." The department believed any such difference proved something had to be unfair.

White people think we can make everyone equal. Other races exert the power we grant them.

If immigrant races fail because we're failing, then maybe we should cease interracial immigration until we get everything right? The best performing education systems in the world are those in racially homogenous countries: not just the pressure cooker of Japan but gentle Finland. That's not to say all racially homogenous countries perform better than those racially diverse, not with some races.

For as long as we refuse to consider that races aren't the same, or that races can't prosper in close proximity to each other, we'll continue tying ourselves up about everything we do. We fret about racism that doesn't exist, and disregard races that do.

That Singaporean Chinese professor addressing Macquarie Graduate School of Management alumni went on to speak of differences between races that aren't matters simply of skin colour. In his observations, Asians succeeded in those industries in which hard work and careful research made small incremental improvements, such as electronics and manufacturing, but failed in those industries requiring imagination, intuition, and inventive leaps into the unknown, such as pharmaceutical industries and the information technologies in which the West excelled.

If he'd been white, his observations would have been racist. Being true would have only made them worse.

When studies suggest differences between races, we don't draw conclusions about race. We draw conclusions about the studies.

In the 1980s, long after the Supreme Court forced integration upon America's public schools, *Time* magazine reported an American study finding that African American children were still generally developing intellectually at a slower rate than white children. For memory, that was by eighteen months to two years. African American and white American children ceased developing at roughly the same age, so that white American adults were generally smarter than African American ones.

The responses, played out in *Time* magazine, were immediate. In our confidence there could be no racial differences, white Americans pilloried the study: the methodology was flawed, the conclusion wrong. We reject results suggesting we're better than other races, calling them Eurocentric. In another reverse twist of logic so characteristic of our postmodern thought, we only know tests are without racial bias when they affirm the racial equality we already believe.

African Americans accepted the results, but blamed them on differing educational opportunities and, of course, white people's racism. They wanted white America to redress their problems.

In 2008, education minister Rod Welford said Queensland's poor results in national literacy and numeracy tests were due to Aboriginal and remote-area students bringing down the state's averages. The ensuing fracas focused upon Aborigines. "I acknowledge the lag associated with indigenous performance," said Aboriginal educationalist Chris Sarra, executive director of the Indigenous Education Leadership Institute, "...the system is failing indigenous kids quite dramatically." Their failure was our fault.

"There is clearly a problem," agreed James Cook University geophysicist Peter Ridd, but the problem wasn't about race. "You have to fix the syllabus."

By 2012, the Florida State Board of Education had given up. It adopted a strategic plan differentiating students by race, aspiring for ninety percent of Asians, eighty-eight percent of whites, eighty-one percent of Hispanics, and seventy-four percent of blacks to be reading at or above grade level by 2018, and ninety-two percent of Asians, eighty-six percent of whites, eighty percent of Hispanics, and seventy-four percent of blacks to be proficient at mathematics. Poverty and disabilities were the subjects of separate objectives.

The Florida Department of Education said the goals were meant to be ambitious but realistic, recognising that different races started from different points. In the 2011 to '12 year, sixty-nine percent of whites, fifty-three percent of Hispanics, and thirty-eight percent of blacks had scored at or above grade level.

Black and Hispanic parents complained to Palm Beach County School Board vice chairwoman Debra Robinson. She said the state board was "proclaiming racism."

We confidently denote other races suffering poorer academic results to be victims of our shortcomings, but sociologist Charles Murray's 1994 book *The Bell Curve* argued that genetics significantly affected intelligence and that black people had lower intelligence. When *New Republic* magazine editor Andrew Sullivan decided to serialise the book, his editorial team threatened to resign. Sullivan only appeased them by publishing nineteen critical responses.

American molecular biologist James Watson was one of two biologists credited in 1953 with discovering the double helix structure of Deoxyribonucleic acid, D.N.A. In 1962, he shared the Nobel Prize in Physiology or Medicine.

In October 2007, Watson told Charlotte Hunt-Grubbe of *The Sunday Times* newspaper that he was "inherently gloomy about the prospect of Africa" because "social policies are based on the fact that their intelligence is the same as ours, whereas all the testing says not really." He dismissed people's hopes that races were equally intelligent because "people who have to deal with black employees find this not true."

In the ensuing uproar, Cold Spring Harbour Laboratory forced Watson to retire as chancellor. In 2014, he became the only Nobel Laureate to sell his Nobel Prize, he said partly because his remarks about race had made him an "unperson," causing him to lose speaking engagements.

Watson was the subject of a 2019 episode of the American television series *American Masters*. The interviewer asked Watson whether he had changed his views about race.

"No, not at all," replied Watson. "I would like for them to have changed, that there be new knowledge which says your nurture is much more important than nature, but I haven't seen any knowledge, and there's a difference on the average between blacks and whites on I.Q. tests." Those tests measured intelligence. "I would say the difference is: it's genetic."

In his 2010 book *Germany Does Itself In*, Bundesbank executive board member Thilo Sarrazin said Germany was being made "*more stupid*" by poorly educated and unproductive Muslim immigrants.

Germany's response wasn't academic. It was to force Sarrazin to resign.

Yet in November 2015, Germany's interior minister Thomas de Maizière announced plans to lower standards at government schools to accommodate refugees and other immigrants. He hoped the lowering would be temporary. Internal documents revealed the government expected eighty-one percent of arrivals in the coming year to have no educational or vocational qualifications at all.

Were we to suspect again that any race was intellectually inferior to ours, I can't imagine us rushing to separate that race from ours. We'd take up a little more of our white people's burden to help, as we did in the nineteenth century. We might worry a little less about mentioning sandwiches.

Soufiane Boufous, a senior research fellow in injury and epidemiology at the George Institute for International Health at the University of Sydney, responded to the stereotype that Asians make poor motorists with a study published in the *Traffic Injury Prevention* journal in 2010. His motivation wasn't to think poorly of anyone, but to help. Without seeming to consider race but place of birth, his research suggested Asian-born drivers were less likely to take risks than Australian-born ones, although he trusted drivers stating whether they took risks. He might have been measuring bravado.

In our determination to see only the best in other races, *The Sydney Morning Herald* newspaper reported the results as meaning Asian drivers were safer and more courteous, but risk aversion isn't the same as being safer. Clinical psychologist Jeroen Decates believed young people who'd grown up in Australia were more likely to break rules and take risks than those from many Asian countries.

"When everyone else says something we are more likely to think it must be true," said Boufous, without any obvious sense he could have been including himself with those words. "We always look for confirmations of our own beliefs."

A speaker to an Australian Corporate Lawyers' Association annual conference in Sydney (early during my time working at Cement Australia) said much the same thing: we interpret our experiences to affirm what we already believe. She was discussing the McDonalds hamburger brand.

People construe evidence in such a way to verify their existing opinions, rather than letting evidence change those opinions. If we think people are the same we see only similarities. If we think people are different, we see differences.

Put another way, colour-blind people don't know that they're colour-blind, even when other people point out to them colours they can't distinguish. When first they're told, they still don't believe those colours are different.

Indian doctor Jayant Patel's negligence was linked to at least eighty-seven deaths at the Bundaberg Base Hospital, Queensland from 2003 until '05. He was trained in India and America.

In each year from 2012 to '15, doctors trained abroad were five times more likely than locally trained doctors to be struck off the British medical register. Indian doctor Umesh Prabhu blamed that on "white decision-makers" in the "institutionally racist" National Health Service.

Syrian doctor Ragheb Nouman said Indian doctors should "clean toilets, not practice medicine," or they'd be the "downfall of the N.H.S." In 2015, he was struck off the medical register.

Sport can reveal all sorts of interesting things about people, if we think about it. Dave Timms, the aged founder of Golden Cross Resources Limited, was a surprising expert on American football. "The black players are the brawn running into each other," he remarked, I think at the lunch the staff shared in place of past Christmas gatherings a couple of days before Christmas 2009; a television set at the Blue Gum Hotel was broadcasting a game between Atlanta and New York. "The ones throwing the ball and setting everything up are the white guys."

A year of three Chinese directors at Golden Cross might've made him think freely of race, although none of the Chinese directors was with us. Old people often say things they shouldn't say; they don't care so much what other people think of their words. They've lived through the time we in the West stopped mentioning such matters. (The less we speak of what's important, the more we speak of what isn't.)

We don't judge races by fields in which we're better, but fields in which we're worse. I think it was in the 1990s that I read an American newspaper headline proclaiming black people to be superior to whites because, as I recall, of black men's successes running short-distance contests, without any particular sportsmen in mind. I imagined the journalists and editors leaping eagerly to their conclusion, publishing it joyfully to the world.

Another guest at my friend Alan's fiftieth birthday party in October 2011 made much the same observation about West African men, because of their athletic performance. He felt frustrated feeling he couldn't talk more about it.

Their impressions were based by reference only to physical prowess in certain sports events. Black women weren't so obviously dominating athletics competitions, although we could blame that upon gender bias. Black men weren't dominating middle and longer distance events; the more solid West Africans perform better in short events and lankier East Africans in longer ones. Black men and women weren't dominating swimming contests, although one commentator dismissed that on the basis fewer black people have access to swimming pools. (Whole oceans haven't made some races better swimmers.)

As black athletes have pointed out, claims of their innate superiority belittle the efforts they make, but more significant than that is the selectivity of it all. None of the disclaimers we apply to dismiss talk of Africans or other races being intellectually inferior to us we apply to talk of them being physically superior, at least to us: discipline, reasons to train, and cultural priorities don't supersede that biology. Not even differences related to dexterity warrant a mention, without being couched in our inferiority.

If it all seems like institutional white racism then it is, but it's racism we doggedly cast against us. Recoiling repulsed at Nazi talk of our racial superiority, we're more comfortable with talk of our supposed racial inferiority. If we reached the same conclusions about particular sports that we do about education, where we reconstruct school syllabuses and examinations trying to obliterate racial differences, we'd restructure sporting programmes and contests.

There is no systemic oppression by white people of other races. There's indulgence. We expend a disproportionate amount of time, money, and effort upon their health, education, and other well-being, because neither they nor we hold them accountable for their shortcomings. Accountability is ours alone.

6. IDEOLOGICALLY
ACCEPTABLE GENERALISATIONS

The Avon Longitudinal Study of Parents and Children examined the lives of more than fourteen thousand mothers who gave birth in 1991 and '92 and their children. It concluded that babies exclusively breastfed for at least the first four weeks of life are more intelligent through their schooling than those fed by bottle from birth.

We're willing to make all manner of generalisations about people, categorising them as we like, provided our generalisations and categorisations don't touch upon race. We accept stereotypes about men with beards, not quite trusting them as we trust clean-shaven men, or mistrusting them even more. (White men are more likely than men of other races to be bearded.)

People who skip breakfast tend to lose their virginity earlier, according to research led by the Japan Family Planning Association and published in 2008. (Researchers must've grown desperate for something to study.) Of course, that was Japan, but the *Agence France-Presse* news service and *News Limited Network* had no qualms reporting it.

There were none of the disclaimers we apply to dismiss research with implications for race. The Japanese study wasn't condemned for being divisive, or rejected for considering matters we knew to be irrelevant. No journalist produced the aging virgin who'd always skipped breakfast, or the teenage harlot who'd always eaten it. No scientist suggested inherent bias in the research, favouring hurried marmalade-eaters over people who patiently sprinkled icing sugar over their strawberries. No politician claimed it was offensive to people born not to eat breakfast or who'd suffered generations of persecution from governments promoting breakfast. Nobody suggested the research made cornflakes feel unwelcome.

In 2015, the University of Innsbruck in Austria published survey results suggesting people who drink their coffee black are more likely to be antisocial or psychopathic. I wondered what races drank black coffee more than white. I think English people are more likely to drink tea, but white.

We merrily investigate brain differences according to political views, but not race. In 2011, Ryota Kanai and three other academics at the University College London published results linking personality traits with specific brain structure. "*We found that greater liberalism was associated with increased grey matter volume in the anterior cingulate cortex*," said the study, "*whereas greater conservatism was associated with increased volume of the right amygdala*." Liberals had more grey matter in a part of the brain associated with uncertainty and conflicts. The conservative brain was bigger in the section more sensitive to threatening situations and that respond with more aggression.

What was unclear was whether physical differences shaped political views, or political views caused physical differences. The study spoke of "political orientation," as if political opinion were something out of a person's control. The research didn't consider, as it wouldn't, whether white people are more liberal and other races more conservative because of physical differences in brains.

The boundaries of our willingness to inquire and research are most interesting. We refuse to investigate brain and other differences between different religions, imagining Nazis doing that. (In fact, Nazi scientists were interested in race, not religion.) Yet, we investigate brain differences between different Christian denominations.

In 2011, researchers Amy Owen and David Hayward at Duke University Medical Centre, North Carolina, reported a correlation between religious practices and changes in the brains of older adults. Protestants who didn't identify as born-again Christians were found to have less atrophy in the hippocampus region than Protestants who did, Catholics, and people with no religious affiliation. Frequency of worship didn't affect brains, but participants who said they'd undergone a religious experience had more atrophy than those who said they hadn't. Other factors affecting hippocampal atrophy, such as age, education, depression or brain size, didn't explain the differences.

Reporting their analysis of the Household, Income Labour Dynamics in Australia Survey in the *Applied Economics Letters* journal in 2011, economists Michael Kortt and Brian Dollery found that Roman Catholic men aged between twenty-five and fifty-four years of age earned six and two thirds percent higher wages than Protestants. There were no statistically significant differences between Protestants and other groups, including those with no religious affiliation.

"That is," said Kortt, "it suggests that being raised a Catholic male might actually instil in a person a series of characteristics such as discipline, which may be rewarded by the labour market." Employers might prefer applicants with surnames sounding Catholic. "They may associate Catholic men with having certain desirable traits such as trustworthiness or a strong work ethic and so on."

The academics also found that the less the men went to church, the more their wages increased (which may be, I suggest, because churchgoers have the work ethic but less of the hunger to chase higher incomes). There was "no evidence that attendance at Catholic school contributes to an earnings premium," although each additional year of schooling added almost ten percent to the wages of Protestant men and six percent for Catholics. Married men enjoyed a wage premium of more than thirteen percent (which could be, I suggest, because women prefer to marry higher income-earning men).

Monash University sociologist Gary Bouma dismissed any interpretation as untested speculation, citing similar data about American wages. "Catholics are much more likely to be urban, thus have access to better educational facilities and to jobs that will be paying money at a slightly higher level."

People's work, wealth, and values can all be subjects of our socially acceptable generalisations. We're categorised by vocation and money: working or not; professional experts or non-professional practitioners; managerial, clerical, farming, or factory; students or teachers. Socio-economic generalisations are all well and good: the places people live and their class. We can call doctors, landlords, and patriots selfish. We can call nurses, tenants, and ourselves not.

Most interestingly to me, we generalise about lawyers, and not just from the portrayals in too many films and television programmes (including ones I've enjoyed watching). Jerry, a consultant to Otter Gold Mines Limited, told me, "You're much nicer as an author than you were as a lawyer." (I don't think he was complimenting me as a writer.)

I read that people have low opinions of lawyers in general in spite of having favourable opinions of individual lawyers they've met. Admittedly, I read that in the *Law Society Journal*.

We make a wealth of generalisations about people. Our generalisations might be true, but truth about race doesn't justify racism.

In 2010, pollster Roy Morgan published the results of his research categorising people by the mobile telephones they used. Apple iPhone users believed computers gave them more control over their lives, loved entertaining at home, but didn't like gardening. L.G. handset users were typically female, aged between fourteen and twenty-four, unlikely to subscribe to pay television, and admitted they weren't mechanically minded. Samsung devotees dressed conservatively, were aged over fifty, avoided air travel, didn't like taking risks, and had an average income of just thirty-four thousand dollars a year. Sony Ericsson owners placed high importance on having full social lives and were fond of fast food. Blackberry users were thirty-five to forty-nine years old, loved electronic mail, earned more than a hundred thousand dollars a year, and regularly saw films, played video games, and read newspapers. They were also the most likely mobile telephone users to have entertained friends and relatives in the past three months.

We're equally comfortable with data describing people by their electronic mail address. Technology website *Hunch* surveyed four hundred and fifty thousand electronic mail users, reporting the results in 2011. A.O.L. and Yahoo! users were most likely overweight women who'd never travelled outside their home countries. Hotmail users were pessimists living in the suburbs. Gmail users were most likely thin, young men aged from eighteen to thirty-four, with college educations, describing themselves as svelte. (I had to check to see what "svelte" meant.) Almost a third of Gmail users said they'd visited more than five countries outside their own, almost twice the proportion of users of Yahoo! and A.O.L.

Employers mightn't have discriminated between job applicants by race, but they did by electronic mail address. A.O.L. addresses made the applicant seem old-fashioned, in spite of A.O.L. users being the most likely to have at least two digital video recorders at home. Fifty-eight percent of them were older than thirty-five. When we get to race, we curl up in a ball.

The first generalisations on the mind of my Hong Kong Chinese friend Ted, sitting among old school friends in a lounge at the Greengate Hotel, the second Thursday evening in August 2011, were about age. "They don't categorise anyone," he told me, thrilled about young people. That might've just been young people within the wealthy Lower North Shore of Sydney, where he and his wife lived and their daughter was a pupil at the prestigious private girls' school, Queenwood. Ted, a past chairman of the Ethnic Communities Council, typified our postmodern vision for a new global elite. "When we were young, we vilified Muslims."

"No, we didn't," I told him; my "we" wasn't his. "We didn't even think about them." I'm not sure I'd thought about Muslims at all until meeting Sunalp at law school.

We had my usual words about me respecting Muslims for retaining religious conviction that the West has lost. "Either Mohammed was God's one true prophet or he wasn't," I told Ted. "Either Jesus was the Son of God, or he wasn't."

"They're just different truths," said Ted.

"We can talk about perception," I told him, "but at the end of the day, either that bar is over there, or it isn't."

Sometime through it all, and I'm not sure why, Ted said: "Muslims are the most honest people."

So we can categorise people, but in a nice way. Having kind things to say is socially acceptable racism and religious generalisation.

Muslim tree loppers I employed at my home were not honest with me. "The evidence seems to be," I told Ted, "based on a recent court case about Muslims raping Christian girls in England, that they treat their own people better than others. They might be honest with their own people, but not with anyone else, and that's better than we are." They have morality among their own Western individuals feel for no one. "We're dishonest with everyone."

"You're a bigot," Ted told me.

To avoid the charge of bigotry, it's not enough to make other races and cultures better than ours. We have to maintain them in perfect esteem.

I'd once thought about asking Ted to review my non-fiction writing to ensure references to Muslims are truthful and fair to Muslims, but I could never compliment them enough to please him. I should've asked Ted to compare honesty between Muslims and Chinese, but only thought of doing so three days after our conversation, writing about it. I could've also said we have different truths, but I could never bring myself to say that.

I couldn't help but recall Ted's words when I read of Ahsan Ali Syed, whose company Western Gulf Advisory defrauded businesspeople from Australia, New Zealand, Malaysia, Ireland, Spain, and the Netherlands of hundreds of millions, perhaps billions, of dollars. He'd previously fled London ahead of bailiffs pursuing unpaid council taxes, leaving behind an unkempt flat and unpaid rent of almost eight thousand pounds. None of his crimes outside the Middle East prevented him appearing on Bahraini television, when his company became sponsor of the Bahraini Supercar series.

The generalisations we like don't need to be true. They're most useful when they're not, helping to combat white racism.

Generalisations were aplenty describing the *"ambitious, industrious immigrants"* in the *Sydney Morning Herald* newspaper article 'City of Cultures' in 2011. The overarching message was that we had no culture in Sydney until the Africans, Asians, Middle Easterners, and Pacific Islanders came. Racial remarks like *"the innate entrepreneurial spirit"* of the Arabs are perfectly acceptable, provided they're positive: our rules of engagement.

Other races also insist upon generalisations about them being positive, caring no more than we care whether they're true. All we need is a nice person of another race to think they're all lovely: that friendly young Islander we met at the art show, the sweet Asian who smiled at us in the film festival, singer Shirley Bassey seemed a terrific lady. We're certain they're tirelessly polite because they are behind delicatessen counters or serving our meals.

Most people of minority races are at their best where their numbers are small or they're otherwise compelled to conform. They're at their worst gathered in groups with the power to act freely.

Nevertheless, we make positive generalisations about other races based on single good experiences or none at all. We infer good things from the best of them, but not bad things from the rest of them.

No number of bad experiences (whether ours or anyone else's) warrants negative generalisations about other races. We could have dozens, hundreds, or even thousands of bad experiences of another race or religion. We still refuse to make negative generalisations about them.

We'll base our ideals upon the best of exceptions before any bad norms, and then insist the best of exceptions are really the norms. It's like dismissing the crimes of the Nazis because Oskar Schindler was good.

No number of exceptions affects our positive generalisations about other races. Just one exception helps us comprehensively demolish negative ones.

We without racism are useless sources of information about other races. Worse than mere ignorance, we're determined to see only the good in other races and disregard the bad. We end up with absurdly jaundiced views.

Anyone wanting to know something about Africans is better asking a Korean than a white person (or anyone from the Ethnic Communities Council). Anyone wanting to learn about Koreans is better asking a Chinaman. My Hong Kong Chinese friend Ted dismissed SsangYong Stavic cars and anything else manufactured by Koreans. We need other races commenting about each other.

Speaking on a television programme broadcast sometime around the year 2000, a South Asian living in Britain contrasted his race seeking to improve their lives by their own initiative, through business, with black West Indians expecting governments to help them. Asians particularly pursue shopkeeping; there came to be a disproportionately high number of Indians working in petrol stations near my home in Sydney (reportedly in breach of their student visas). East Asians work in fast-food restaurants. Asians retain a purpose we've lost. We're only interested in racism.

7. SPECIESISM

"We shall never be rough or heartless where it is not necessary; that is clear," Heinrich Himmler, *Reichsführer* of the *Schutzstaffel*, told about a hundred group leaders in Posen, occupied Poland, the first Monday of October, 1943. "We Germans, who are the only people in the world who have a decent attitude to animals, will also adopt a decent attitude to these human animals."

Himmler wasn't the only person to ascribe to Germans what could've been much of Europe, but the *Schutzstaffel* carried out the Holocaust. He was instructing the perpetrators of Holocaust to avoid unnecessary suffering by the Jews and other victims. Apart from being an intriguing construction of what a decent attitude could be, Himmler's words blurred the distinction between people (well, some people) and animals.

Having discarded our racial identities since then, there's no end of biological identities we can discard. We no longer want race (least of all our own) and, bogged down with abstraction, aren't too sure about species (least of all our own).

Among the Jews killed in the Holocaust were the grandparents of philosopher Peter Singer, born in Melbourne after his parents fled Austria in 1938. I first heard his name during my philosophy lectures at Macquarie University. I think it was the course textbook that called him Australia's only philosopher. If that seemed harsh on Australia, then at least we had one. America mightn't have produced any, but she attracted them. Singer became a bioethics professor at Princeton University.

Through such books as *Animal Liberation* and *Should the Baby Live*, Singer categorised apes, dogs, and other animals as non-human persons, redefining a person so he or she needn't be human. He categorised disabled children and old people as human non-persons, redefining a human so he or she needn't be a person. Our budding ideology of animal rights arose not from our love of animals, but our contempt for people (well, some people).

Upholding the sanctity of human life any more than other life is speciesism, a term coined by British psychologist Richard Ryder in 1973, while lying in the bath. (Not that he spent the whole year lying in the bath.) *It was like racism or sexism,* he wrote, *prejudice based upon morally irrelevant physical differences.* (By morally, he should have said ideologically.)

Speciesism and racism become different degrees of discrimination. Our Western rejection of race makes species untenable.

For those of us who haven't married our cat, dog, or pot plant (and even if we have), our families aren't just racist. They're speciesist.

In a rare instance of the postmodern West caring about our ancestors, Ryder saw rejecting racism and speciesism as the logical conclusion of morality since Charles Darwin theorised all species had common ancestors. (Those ancestors might be amino acids on an embryonic planet.) Yet, there is no such logical conclusion from Darwin's theories of evolution. Nor was one imagined until after the Holocaust.

Darwin himself was a racist and speciesist, interpreting the past and future as contests for survival between races and species. Since the Holocaust, we've rejected such contests. Instead, we're inclusive.

People who cite Darwin's theories to rebuke Biblical Creationism (and even Christianity, in spite of Darwin's belief in God) don't mention his pronouncements on race. Creationists like American industrial chemist Russell Grigg also pursued inclusion, rejecting contests between peoples, but that's about all he had in common with Ryder. Writing in 2006, Grigg believed the logical conclusion from Darwin's theories wasn't the end of racism and speciesism but the Holocaust, euthanasia, ethnic cleansing, stem cell embryo research, and abortion of deformed babies.

Such a link would have been a surprise to many of the people involved, although linking race to babies explains why we don't bear babies anymore. Speciesists tolerate euthanasia and abortion of deformed babies.

Ryder and Grigg offered two diametrically opposed lines of reasoning. One rejected racism and speciesism, because of Darwin. The other rejected Darwin, because of his racism. Both began with the Holocaust and worked backwards.

Yet, being speciesist doesn't make me want to harm or kill

animals recklessly. I don't want cows to suffer before they become my tenderloin steaks, any more than I want broccoli or mashed potatoes to suffer.

Besides, all species and even all humans might not have common ancestors; we might not all be related. Many different amino acids (or whatever) might've become living beings, those million millennia ago.

The more comfortable we become being speciesist, would argue Ryder and Singer, the more comfortable we become being racist. If one division is arbitrary, then so is another.

Tom White, director of the Centre for Ethics and Business at Loyola Marymount University, Los Angeles, focused on individuality. "We're saying the science has shown that individuality, consciousness, and self-awareness are no longer unique human properties," he told the annual meeting of the American Association for the Advancement of Science in Vancouver in 2012, talking to Western individualism. (He didn't imagine the lack of individuality among other races, or even among white people anymore.)

Human rights being a Western invention post-Holocaust, so are animal rights. White was promoting a ten-point declaration of rights for cetaceans, including dolphins, whales, and porpoises. (If dolphins are so smart, I wonder why none of them learn to write, although that's not a point of differentiation we apply to humans either.) Their rights included "life, liberty, and well-being," along with freedom of movement, residence in their natural environment, and protection against "disruption of their cultures." (It's more than we have.)

"Dolphins are non-human persons," White explained, as Singer would've said. "A person needs to be an individual, and if individuals count, then the deliberate killing of individuals of this sort is ethically the equivalent of deliberately killing a human being. The captivity of beings of this sort, particularly in conditions that would not allow for a decent life, is ethically unacceptable..."

Western individualism has no logical boundaries in biology but only in being individuals; replacing biology with ideology means we replace one line of discrimination with another. Solitary salmon would have rights. Schools of whitebait would not. It's animal individualism.

"This case is on the next frontier of civil rights," said lawyer

Jeffrey Kerr in 2012, of his five clients' suit before Judge Jeffrey Miller in San Diego alleging slavery by Sea World. Those clients were orcas: what we used to call killer whales (until that became defamatory).

The People for the Ethical Treatment of Animals organisation, which filed the case, claimed treating animals as property was the same argument used against African Americans and women before granting them constitutional rights. (Neither Africans nor women seemed upset by the comparison.)

"This is a historic day," said Kerr. "For the first time in our nation's history, a federal court heard arguments as to whether living, breathing, feeling beings have rights and can be enslaved simply because they happen to not have been born human."

We've belittled birth to a circumstance, which we did when we rejected race. We aren't fundamentally what we are because we came into being as we are, but quite apart from the being we were born. It's as if we were all once spirits queued up waiting to be born. This one became a Dutchman. The next became a flea.

Like other rights before them, animal rights are becoming the norm through the compliant West. In 2007, a region of Spain voted to give legal human rights to apes.

Other races have taken more to expecting and even demanding Western rights than they've taken to granting them, but they have no interest to take this one up. Animals neither demand nor even realise they have the rights we accord them.

We don't excuse racism because of the behaviour of other races. We don't excuse speciesism because of the behaviour of other species.

Ten years after Arab terrorists destroyed the World Trade Centre in New York killing three thousand people, officers at the memorial's security system were ordered to examine surveillance tapes. They weren't looking for terrorists, but for police officers who'd laughed at a brown and orange pigeon.

"Your appearance in public has to be professional," a police supervisor admonished officers at the First Precinct station house, during eight o'clock roll calls the mornings of the second Thursday and Friday of December, 2011. "We're receiving complaints about police officers' demeanour regarding a bird..."

The pigeon hated other birds, aggressively evicted them from its territory, was hostile to police, and defecated on an officer's companion. None of that justified police officers not respecting it. "But then someone saw us playing around with the bird and complained," said a police officer. "So now we can't really have anything to do with him."

Americans must show their respect to pigeons. Swiss must allow fish their discretion. By 2008, Switzerland required aquariums to have at least one opaque wall to ensure privacy for the fish.

The Swiss are extraordinarily sensitive to the feelings of fish. Swiss law forbid goldfish from being flushed down toilets unless they'd been anaesthetised.

The sanctity we give other lives extends way beyond animals. If intelligence is the bar, it's a very low bar.

My parents, sisters, and I were at my Aunt Betty's home in Berry around about 1980 when one of us found a leech on his or her skin. My father wanted some salt to pour on it, but my aunt refused him. "That's only if you want to kill it," she told him.

During a televised interview, America's President Barack Obama upset the People for the Ethical Treatment of Animals by killing a fly. Being Obama, spokesman Bruce Friedrich's criticism was muted. He said "swatting a fly on TV indicates he's not perfect." It sent Obama a device for catching flies and releasing them outside.

I wasn't surprised. A long time earlier, I'd watched the 1994 American film *The Shawshank Redemption*. The story of a man unjustly confined for decades in gaol didn't concern the American Humane Association so much as another prisoner in the film feeding a live maggot to a crow he kept. The film-makers thus found a maggot that died of natural causes.

Live maggots have rights that dead maggots have relinquished. We don't confer rights on dead people either. If we did, we mightn't be so quick to damn our forebears for doing what they believed was right.

The American Humane Association rated the 1989 film *The Abyss* as "unacceptable" because of a scene in which a rat was submerged in oxygenated liquid, although director James Cameron was adamant the rat suffered no harm. The scene was edited out of the British version of the film, because the Royal Veterinarian was concerned the rat found it painful.

In our pursuit of equality, we're trivialising differences between animals, people, and plants. A maggot is no less alive than a weed in the garden. Cranberries were no less a life form than the roast turkey they accompany. In 2008, an ethics committee commissioned by the Swiss parliament interpreted constitutional amendments passed a decade earlier as requiring scientists performing experiments to treat plants with dignity.

I didn't understand what that meant. I still don't.

Even a division into life forms based on carbon and derived from amino acids is discriminatory. A plant in the garden is no less alive than a virus in the blood. By the rest of our reasoning, viruses and bacteria should have the same rights as at least some animals and human beings. Saving a person from infection can mean killing virus and bacteria, but they have as much rights to infect our bodies as we have to occupy our bodies; anything else would be virophobic or bacteriophobic. We become cohabitants. They might kill us, but we prefer to die than discriminate.

In 2005, Richard Ryder introduced a new moral measure he called painism: there should be no discrimination against anything capable of feeling pain. We can only discriminate against "rocks and rivers and houses."

Using pain as a measure is no less arbitrary than anything else. We already ascribe sensitivities to maggots and plants that mightn't feel pain.

Why need a being be alive? While walking through Sydney city early in the 1990s (I think) with our younger sister beside her, the elder of my two sisters paused at a huge building site. Excavators were carving into sandstone. As melodramatic as she could be, she stretched out her arms and screamed at the construction workers, "Save the rocks!"

Rejecting speciesism requires us to be cannibals, vegetarians, or starving. The only boundaries about which we're certain are those around our individual selves, but even those come to fade.

In December 2011, Dutch television presenters Dennis Storm and Valerio Zeno allowed surgeons to remove flesh from their buttocks and abdomen respectively, which a chef then cooked. They then ate each other's meat. Their cannibalism wasn't for a Christmas party but entertainment for television audiences, broadcast on their programme *Proefkonijnen*, meaning guinea pigs. Rejecting all other discriminations requires us to eat ourselves.

Replacing the arbitrariness of biological definitions of people with the arbitrariness of ideological definitions doesn't make life easier for other races and species. It makes ours more precarious.

Ethicists Alberto Giubilini and Francesca Minerva, writing in the *Journal of Medical Ethics* in 2011, defined a person *"to mean an individual who is capable of attributing to her own existence some (at least) basic value such that being deprived of this existence represents a loss to her."* A moral right to life, they argued, depended on it. Thus mature animals have rights to life. We should be free to kill newborn human babies.

We were never more callous than we've become since we rejected our racism, because our rejection of racism wasn't a rejection of violence. We just moved the markers by which we're willing to kill.

The District of Columbia's Wildlife Protection Act of 2010 prohibited pest control companies killing rice rats or deer mice. Pest controllers had to capture them, ideally in families, and transfer them to wildlife rehabilitators (whatever they are). The prohibition didn't apply to other species of rats. We discriminate between rodents as we don't between people.

The fourth Friday in September 2011, my wife, two of our daughters, and I attended Ku-ring-gai Council chambers, where researcher Mal Weerakoon spoke of a plan under way to use native bush rats to keep black rats away from the Sydney Harbour foreshore. The two species of rats could interbreed but, unlike people of different races, never had. (Animals discriminate.)

Most of the twenty-six people in the audience were willing to kill black rats if we could do so humanely, because of the threat they posed to native rats and other native animals. (I'd used rat traps whatever the rats, but thought better than mentioning it.) It was rat racism and rat nationalism to be sure, although applying the same to people would've been inconceivable.

That wasn't the most intriguing sense to come from the room. One man in the audience, appearing around about sixty-five years of age, picked up on Weerakoon's remarks about black rats in urban areas feeding primarily from garbage scraps and pet food left out. "Have you thought about getting rid of us?" he asked, without smiling.

Nobody laughed. His was no joke.

"There's twenty million of us," replied Weerakoon, referring to the population of Australia at the time.

The man who'd asked the question, born about the time of the

Second World War, remained unperturbed. By his appearance and that of the people sitting with him, he was Jewish. "It's been done before."

If speciesism is morally equivalent to racism, so distinguishing ourselves from other species is like distinguishing ourselves from other races, then distinguishing ourselves from other races isn't so bad. If we equate racism with speciesism and speciesism is rational, then racism is rational.

8. HUMANISING ANIMALS

In the 2007 American film *Ratatouille*, food critic Anton Ego didn't like people. He preferred food, but didn't merely like food. He *loved* it.

With ambitions to be a great chef, Remy resolved his struggle between identifying as a rat or a person by deciding he was neither. He was a cook. (Our model New Western Person had become New Western Creature.) The film spurred sales of rats as pets.

"A rat is a pig is a dog is a boy," said Ingrid Newkirk, founder of People for the Ethical Treatment of Animals, in 1989. (I won't ever eat a casserole she's made. Nor do I want to imagine her boyfriend.)

In spite of our growing rejection of speciesism, humanising animals hasn't led us to sense in ourselves the instincts to herd and procreate that we respect in animals; equating humans to animals has its limits. "I'm not only uninterested in having children," said Newkirk in 2003, "I am opposed to having children. Having a pure-bred human baby is like having a pure-bred dog; it is nothing but vanity, human vanity."

Caring nothing for the pedigree of people, pet owners care about the pedigree of pets. It makes them look rich.

We confuse self-respect and self-love with vanity. Equating animals to humans meant Newkirk didn't like either of them.

Losing sight of species, gender remains. *"Set a Sister Free,"* said Australian television personality Michelle Bridges for the Royal Society for the Prevention of Cruelty to Animals in March 2015, referring to a hen. She wanted people to buy eggs from free-range chickens without cages.

In 2008, the European Court agreed to hear a British schoolteacher's claim for the court to declare Mathew a person so she could adopt him. Mathew was twenty-six years old, which was rather old to be adopted, except that Mathew was a chimpanzee.

Without children to accord human names, we give them to animals. We even afford them gender-specific names that many of our children no longer enjoy. Traditional pet names would deny us the pretence that our pets are people.

Calling ourselves pet owners confess our pets have little say in the matter. We thus became their companions, custodians, or primary caregivers, much like mothers or fathers. In 2013, Virgin Australia announced a frequent flyer programme for pets.

"*Life is better with pets,*" read the large scrolled lettering to what seemed at first like a bright and frilly community announcement, one Saturday night in 2009. (I didn't normally pay much attention to advertisements, but I watched community announcements.) My eldest son and I were watching the film *Collateral*, with me trying not to notice the irritating television station watermark in the corner of the screen, but there was no watermark for community announcements and commercials. I wondered who promoted pets as we watched the images of a happy couple welcoming and being welcomed by a huge dog, before seeing, "*Pets are better with Supercoat.*"

The advertiser was Purina. "*Your pet, our passion,*" I read afterwards.

("*Life is better with children,*" would be a real community announcement, but perhaps parents don't need to hear it. More likely, we're frightened of unsettling people without children. Companies selling baby products only hint to people already parents, "*Your children, our passion.*")

Marie (pronounced Mah-rie, aristocratically), my secretary at Otter Gold Mines Limited, was pretty but painfully thin, with well-defined muscles stretched along her suntanned arms and legs. She was taller than most women and held her head, shoulders, and neck high among her colleagues at the office. Her long fingers struck her computer keys and the screen transfixed her eyes.

She offered to work on weekends without hesitation, couriering parcels to the airport. During the week, she remained working studiously at her desk rather than join birthday cake celebrations or Friday night drinks only a few metres away. Focussed on her chores, Marie rarely countenanced social conversations or interaction unrelated to work.

For five years, for reasons only Marie knew, she'd refused to speak to Ros. That might have been because Ros was a mother. It wasn't, I think, for Ros being the human resources manageress.

Marie had tried to bear children but, without them, fretted for her husband as might a mother. She was also the proud custodian of two small Maltese dogs, Harry and Lucas. Returning to the office after shopping at lunchtime one day, she struggled to carry a massive white plastic bag. Inside the bag were two big blue and yellow plastic balls. Pets were her babies that never grow up.

Her few sociable conversations normally involved her talking of her "boys," while I politely listened. "You're not really interested are you," she once said.

"Yes," I lied. Pets are complications.

Standing before my desk in my office, I think in another brief conversation, Marie remarked matter-of-factly, "You have to take care of yourself. You can't let anything happen to you." She was referring to me being a parent.

"Don't you think that you also have reasons to take care of yourself?" I asked her.

"Not the way that you do."

Whether she envied or pitied me, the unimportance she gave her life disturbed me. If I could've said anything to make her value her life more than she did then I would've said it, but I didn't know what to say. Hers was a right to risk her life I didn't want.

Animals and the diseases they might carry were forbidden from the offices at which I'd worked, until I worked for Golden Cross Resources Limited. The office manageress occasionally brought to the offices her fidgety little dogs: brown-haired Jackson; white-haired Bo. They scarpered around underfoot, but nobody seemed to mind. Unpleasant people were conspicuously kind to the dogs.

My Jewish friend Ian Biner considered writing a book of stories for people to read to their pets. He was a good writer, so I hoped the stories weren't written "meow, meow" or "woof, woof-woof," and the storylines weren't too species-specific.

The differences between people and animals are most obvious not in matters of hate but love. Pets respond to sentiment with sentiment, remaining with us for food and shelter. We pretend to relate with them, even to love and be loved by them. They can be the illusion of relationship and even adoration without commitment, challenge, or anything being said we don't want to hear. They preserve our centres of small universes another person might unsettle; pets are friends for people no longer relating to people. They're the longings of people frightened of being alone; lonely owners concoct conversations with creatures that can't understand.

Our affection for pets makes people superfluous. During a holiday at my father's home, my twelve-year-old eldest son encountered what my stepmother called her "child in dog form" she called by the Italian name Sabbia. She cuddled, played with, and loved it.

When my eldest son referred to it as "it," she objected. She insisted it was "he," or sometimes "she." Names that aren't gender-specific can be a problem.

Once our opposition to speciesism really takes hold, I expect speaking of children will fall away too. They might be life forms, before that falls away too.

Before the dog, my stepmother owned a black rabbit: Floppy. Before the rabbit, she was matron and guardian of another dog. She took the dog to yoga classes on a yoga mat to keep it from being stressed, but still one day it suddenly bailed her and her daughter up in their home.

That threat of attack, although no one was hurt, led my stepmother (and the dog, I presume) to consult a dog psychiatrist. Whether the dog barked at cards with inkblots or the psychiatrist laid the dog on a couch and asked it to bark about its puppyhood, I don't know. In any event, the psychiatrist decided the dog had reverted to its natural instincts: its ancient genetic recesses before human beings domesticated dogs. In a pack of wild dogs, it would've been innately the leader.

The psychiatrist was unable to treat it (if indeed a psychiatrist can treat anyone or anything). My stepmother had the animal put down. We talk freely of killing people, but euphemise killing animals to speak of putting them down.

We struggle when domesticated animals revert to their natural instincts. We struggle when people do, too.

Leaving us free of the responsibilities that loving people can bring, pets can be bought at a whim and ask little of us. If we tire of them, as we tire of most things, we can sell them, give them away, or abandon them by a river. As often as not, we'd sooner abandon everyone else.

We let pets prevail over children. On the first Monday morning in June 2010, British grandmother Mandy Hands and her son Ashley woke from their sleep in their home in Coventry to find their home on fire. Quickly, they escaped with their dogs, forgetting eleven-year-old Curtis asleep in a spare bedroom.

Firefighters rescued her grandson, Ashley's son, later. At least she was embarrassed about it.

In our neighbourhood, cats and more often dogs lounge about our lawns while their owners are otherwise engaged, dogs wander through any door left open. When our local newspaper printed a letter from a resident complaining that dogs wandering through her neighbourhood defecated on her lawns, dog owners were indignant. Did the letter writer not understand, the dog owners asked, how much pleasure their dogs gave them? That might be, a resident retorted, but they weren't *her* dogs.

We've made not just the wilderness but our towns and cities the animal kingdom. Several local council areas in Sydney have set aside parks for dogs to run around unleashed, in spite of parents fearing that unleashed dogs threatened their children. "Perhaps," said one pet owner in 2008, "if more children learned how to treat and relate kindly to dogs, and animals in general, these very infrequent attacks would cease altogether."

The New South Wales government agreed. It spent more than four million dollars educating people how to "interact safely with dogs and prevent bites." The amount was piffling aside the billions of dollars pet owners spend buying, feeding, housing, treating, decorating, shampooing, grooming, and generally pampering their pets (not to mention consulting dog psychiatrists).

Another pet owner didn't just want parks set aside for dogs to run about unleashed. He or she wanted children put on leashes and gags affixed to their mouths, "so they can't scream and annoy my dogs" and "so they can't put their grubby, little mitts near my clean dogs."

Animals unleashed aren't as bad as their owners unleashed. "Leash-free parks encourage dogs to socialise and…be better citizens," claimed another pet owner. (I have no idea what makes any animal a good citizen; we're not sure what makes a person a good citizen, anymore.) "Dogs never annoy anyone quite like kids can, running around, screaming, and carrying on, spreading their germs to everyone else. At least pets don't spread disease!" (Australia was free of rabies in dogs.)

Dog owners opposed fences protecting children from the dogs. "*A fence causes offence to our dogs,*" said one protester's banner. (With people so quick to feel offence, we think animals are too.)

Another dog owner berated a mother whose child was hitting a plastic golf ball, because the ball was a choking hazard to his dog. To the parents who complained about dog faeces, yet another dog owner retorted: "Dog bacteria is good for children."

Throughout these conflicts unimaginable with other races and religions, dog owners denigrated people with children for being breeders. (They weren't concerned about breeding dogs.) Emboldened in their cause along the way to getting the parks free of leashes they wanted in the Ku-ring-gai Municipality, dog owners threatened the lives of councillor Adrienne Ryan's two daughters: the daughters of a past New South Wales police commissioner, Peter Ryan.

Equating people to animals hasn't meant treating animals better. It means treating human beings worse.

English courts long ago allowed organisations helping animals to be charities on the basis that kindness to animals would make people kinder to each other. That reasoning no longer applies. People who like people can also like animals, but the reverse is much rarer. While we became more and more callous with our compatriots and brusque with waiters and staff, we smiled ever more sweetly at small animals, birds, and fish.

We care more about animals than people. I think it was during the Asia Pacific summit of the World Economic Forum in Melbourne in September 2000 that protesters knocked down a police horse, Hollywood. The Australian public feared more for its fate than that of the policewoman who'd been riding it, confined to hospital with her injuries.

In our desire to protect animals, the value we ascribe animals became not just the equal of people. It exceeds it.

Sometime around about 2002, an Australian court (I think it was) imposed fines upon a man who'd attacked three police officers and a police dog, but the fine for cruelty to the dog was three times the fines for assaulting each of the officers. An appeals court reduced the fines, so that the fine for cruelty to the dog was only twice that for assaulting each officer.

In 2015, I dismissed the warning by a group of computer experts known collectively as the Future of Life Institute that robots could use human beings as pets (if we're lucky) when they achieve superintelligence. They were being robotist.

Our rejection of our species is our rejection of our race. It all harks back to our determination not to discriminate by physical difference.

The last Friday of October 2010, my eldest daughter wanted a pet axolotl: her latest fixation for the moment. "Axolotls are fish with special needs," I told my children with me in the car.

My daughter replied, "You're racist."

9. RACIAL NATURES

Ours is the wonderful West, where children are no longer punished for much for fear of harming their fragile self-esteem and because we're not judgemental. The Education and Care Services National Acts, passed in 2011 by Australian state and territory governments, restricted childcare centres in disciplining bad children. "Staff need to sit with children and talk through the situation," said Early Childhood Australia chief Pam Cahir.

Children hitting other children were no longer being naughty. It was just a situation.

We worry about race. Eagerly we distribute images of two children from different races hugging each other and think that means racism is learned, but they are two children in the absence of others. The point about tribalism is that it is in the context of groups, separating those of the tribe from those not of the tribe. Interaction between two solitary individuals is individualism, without others at play.

When they were young, my daughters preferred to play with white dolls in stores. When observers from the Centre for Equity and Innovation in Early Childhood at the University of Melbourne noticed that white girls in Melbourne preschools in 2003 were more likely to play with white dolls than other dolls, they wouldn't have a bar of it. Revelations of racist babies led educators to devise strategies to weed white children four and five years old from white dolls. No one seemed to notice whether children of colour also played with dolls of their colours.

We'd made black and Asian dolls not just to cater to black and Asian children, but to be the dolls of white children. Aboriginal, South Asian, and African children are free to favour their dolls looking much like white dolls.

There are no old-fashioned black golliwogs with hair, clothes, and cushion stuffing suggesting that racial differences might be more than skin tone. Calling them golliwogs was altogether too much difference, although their biggest problem was coming from the time of our old-fashioned racism.

In her last year of preschool, my youngest daughter and other children in the red room made life-size pictures of themselves. The children sat and lay on white paper and drew outlines of each other, which I presume the teachers then cut out before the children painted them. The children drew a myriad of colours, lines, shapes, and patterns not recognisable as any human being, or anything much else, except perhaps to the most devoted and imaginative of parents. At the classroom meeting with the few parents that came along, one of the two red-room teachers explained the activity to us. "They get to see how different they all are," said Fiona. "Some are short. Some are tall. Some are fat. Some are thin."

Fiona listed many areas of difference between the children, without talk of race among them. I'd collected my daughter there often enough to know there were several Asians in the class: Chinese, Koreans, and Indians, in particular. There mightn't have been as many different colours of skin in the children as there were different colours of paint in the pictures, but only in the last area of difference between those children did Fiona hint a little of race. "Some of them have black hair."

We think that if we don't mention race, nobody will notice. If people no longer notice, we think race no longer exists.

It does. Children notice.

"We know that by preschool, children show in-group bias concerning race," said University of Washington psychologist Jessica Sommerville in 2014, after she and Harvard University researcher Monica Burns published results of research showing natural racism in fifteen-month-old babies. "The findings imply that infants can take into account both race and social history when deciding which person would make a better playmate."

"Babies are sensitive to how people of the same ethnicity as the infant, versus a different ethnicity, are treated," said Burns. What matters is loyalty, not justice. "They weren't just interested in who was being fair or unfair."

Sommerville preferred not to label babies as racist, but that was because of her understanding of racism. "Racism connotes hostility," she said, "and that's not what we studied." She nevertheless said that the study showed that babies use basic distinctions, including race, to "cleave the world apart by groups of what they are and aren't a part of." Race is intrinsic to babies encountering people of other races: to the way human beings see each other.

My inescapable sense from observations though my life is that, for all the differences between people, we have some common instincts. They're no less natural when we try so hard to escape them. Among them is that, amidst our human nature, we yearn to feel part of something; our tribal instincts remain. Paradoxically perhaps, any identity less than the whole of human existence lets people be part of a group. We're innately tribal: some people are our people and some people aren't. It's more than a desire to be part of a herd less than every human or living being on earth. It's a sense that, in some definitive way, we already are.

Our natural prejudices are for people like us. In 2010, Salvatore Maria Aglioti, a cognitive and social neuroscientist at the Sapienza University in Rome, published his studies of Africans and Italians in the journal *Current Biology*. He found that people don't empathise with those from other races. They empathise with their own.

People also empathise with imaginary people with violet skin. Aglioti thought that meant we learnt racism, although it might mean we're still trying our best to be inclusive of other races, in spite of our knowledge of those races we've already encountered. (Reality teaches us something.)

Tribalism and preserving the tribe are natural, keeping outsiders at a distance. Western individualism is unnatural, multiracialism even more so.

Social neuroscientist Joan Chiao at Northwestern University in Evanston, Illinois, thought it could make evolutionary sense that we feel less empathy for people different to us. "In case of war or even a friendly competition like a football game, it could be adaptive to feel less empathy for people we consider our opponents."

Racial homogeneity allows empathy among tribesmen and women, giving rise to altruism between them. As regards our own, said Chiao, "it also makes evolutionary sense for us to feel the pain of others, as it might cue that there is danger close by. Also, without feeling the pain of others, it could be harder to motivate altruistic behaviours, especially if such behaviours come at a cost."

Within a family, tribe, or race there can be heroism. Among the newspaper stories to identify a person as Aboriginal was one about the man who drowned saving the life of a distant cousin with whom he was swimming in the Darling River at Bourke, New South Wales, the first Friday in November 2011. He made an interesting contrast with the man in the Macquarie River at Dubbo the previous Sunday, who drowned trying to save a dog.

Western individuals don't feel each other's pain. Little wonder then we've lost much of our altruism, at least for each other.

Ross Gittins was economics editor for the *Sydney Morning Herald* newspaper, but his focus upon economics didn't deter him from recognising human instincts. *"Considering the human animal's deep-seated fear of foreigners,"* he wrote in 2010, *"it's not surprising resentment has focused on immigration."*

Discrimination isn't just natural. It's desirable.

In 2011, psychologists Catherine Cottrell at the University of Florida and Steven Neuberg at Arizona State University associated human prejudice with living in groups. Groups are beneficial for survival, enjoying protection from others, shelter, collecting food and water, as well as finding mates and caring for children. Conversely, groups are wary of outsiders who could harm the group by spreading disease, stealing resources, or killing or hurting individuals. We're wary of people not part of our tribe.

Prejudice needn't be overt or intentional. Implicit Association Test results carried out by psychologists have long found prejudices against outsiders to be innate to humans, even among people caring deeply about equality (as we in the West do). Forever pursuing more means of trying to override our natural racism, those tests suggested that encouraging people to take an outsider's perspective reduces their prejudice. The outsider's perspectives don't need to be real; they can be social constructs. We lose *our* perspectives.

Also trying to erase racism was psychologist and researcher Gordon Hodson at Brock University, Ontario in 2012. He reported that even people claiming not to have racial prejudice held unconscious racial biases he called "underground" racism. Alluding to the problems we all face when different races come together, even if we blithely deny them, he noted "recent research demonstrating that intergroup contact is mentally challenging and cognitively draining." By group, he meant race.

Becoming blind to race doesn't happen naturally. We need to work at it. Instead of respecting our racial natures, we set about obliterating natural racism with gusto; we're not in the slightest bit interested in prejudiced perspectives. We'd rather try to make people what we think civilised beings should be, as there's never before been attempted among democracies, than cater to instincts we consider aren't civilised. Knowing that racism is a natural human instinct doesn't deter us. It inspires us to strive harder.

From 2002 onwards, the British government required teachers to monitor children for racism and report all racist incidents to their local authorities. The reports named the alleged perpetrators and victims, described the incidents, and set out the punishment. These weren't mere situations like children hitting each other, which adults and innocent children are supposed only to discuss, but wrongdoings for which naughty children were to be punished, whatever the impact upon their self-esteem.

While children could kill other children without suffering criminal records into their adulthood, records of their racism or other discriminatory behaviour were passed from one school to another whenever children changed schools. They could be used if potential employers or universities asked the schools for references about them.

For their part, the local authorities monitored the numbers of racist and other discriminatory incidents. They searched for any patterns and took measures to redress them. So certain are we that children are racist, they refused to accept school principals saying there'd been no incidents of racism at their schools, criticising them for under-reporting.

The result was thirty thousand schoolchildren being reported for racist and other discriminatory incidents in England and Wales in the 2008 to '09 year. Thirty-four thousand were reported the following year, including more than twenty thousand in primary schools and some no more than three years of age in nursery schools. They included a youngster accused of being racist for calling a boy "broccoli head." (Perhaps the school imagined green vegetables were a race.) If the system wasn't eradicating all hints of racism, then it was getting better at identifying where they might linger.

The British government sponsored the National Children's Bureau, which in 2008 released a guide three hundred and sixty-six pages long, longer than most books, *Young People and Racial Justice*. Acknowledging that young people had the ability to "*recognise different people in their lives,"* it was determined to destroy that ability. Minds open to reality and expression, we close. It wanted adults to reprimand children for racism, condemn them in clear specific terms, and report them to their local council.

Extraordinarily thorough, the bureau believed racism wasn't manifest just by making insensitive remarks and name-calling, but in describing people as *"those people"* and young children forming relationships with children from their own race. (We're not supposed to do that.) Even small children not liking foreign food were displaying racism. (Presumably, ham and pork are exempt from that concern.) They can smash windows and receive no more than counselling, but if they don't gobble down curries and beg for some more, we tear them apart.

The bureau didn't seem to care if immigrant children don't like English food. English people don't like English food anymore, at least that they're willing to admit. Trying to inculcate unnatural empathies, we fail to keep natural empathies.

There's no limit to our determination to eradicate race. The bureau advised adults to include toddlers and babies in their efforts to combat racism.

The time might come that an ultrasound examination of a pregnant woman's womb will seek signs of racism. The foetus might flinch in response to a foreign food the mother ate. There may be a flicker when the immigrant doctor is a little too rough examining her. It might be enough that the baby is white.

It all seems to work. Colours children see slowly fade. Refusing to see colours, or colourlessness, children change, or at least claim to have changed. We keep denying human nature or trying to change it. Where we can't change human nature, we suppress it. We have the arrogance and stupidity to think we should rise above it.

Rather than forming relationships within our race, we form no relationships at all. That's individualism.

Racism needn't be hatred or bigotry. When my son and two elder daughters enrolled in our local primary school, they saw Mister Hulley's skin was brown. At the time, he was the only male teacher at the school, which my wife assured me was enough to get excess attention from girls. (We weren't yet so focused on eradicating gender, too.) It didn't deter Mister Hulley from pointing to my eldest daughter and, with a rhythmic long song from the syllables of her name, saying "Estherrrr!"

My children liked him, without ignoring his race. Unaware of what adults expected of them, whenever my two elder daughters saw a dark-skinned man at the shops or walking along a footpath, they called him "Mister Hulley Two," or "Mister Hulley Three," and so forth. They laughed as they did, as they often laughed. Few of the men overheard my daughters' words. Those that did seemed not to mind. My daughters went so far and further than "Mister Hulley Twenty-Seven," or some number like that, although I think they'd lost track of what numbers they'd reached.

Of all the observations the children could make of a person, none could so much as allude to race. My eldest daughter's teacher in years five and six, the teacher the children called Mrs Lounge, asked each child in the class to describe a picture of a boy with dark skin. My daughter replied: "The boy has dark skin…"

"Racist!" Mrs Lounge scolded her.

Not all the parents were so fond of Mister Hulley, as not all parents are fond of any teacher, no more the good teachers than the bad. Some parents lobbied the Department of Education to transfer him from the school, but the department paid little attention to parents. It paid attention to teachers. When Mister Hulley complained to the department about those parents' treatment of him and wanted the transfer, the department obliged.

Sometime after Mister Hulley left the school, my elder daughters wanted every extensively marketed Bratz doll in the series; being good consumers, just one or two wasn't enough. The gaudy dolls came with extensive fashion accessories in silver-painted and other plastic: tall shoes, short skirts, bits of tinsel. It didn't matter to my daughters that the dolls came in every major race, although I'm sure it mattered to the dolls' designers.

Trying to change human nature, there's a constant tension around us. The evening before Good Friday 2010, I was with most of my children at our local supermarket buying food for Easter. Unfortunately, all the hot cross buns had been sold, but there was still fish and other seafood to buy. My eldest daughter stopped at the shelves at the end of an aisle and, without thought of Easter, picked up a cup of flavoured noodles.

"We're not buying Asian food," I told her.

"You're racist!" she told me, unconcerned by the strangers around us, including the Asians. "You're racist if you don't like

Asian food."

10. DISCRIMINATION

"That's discrimination!" is a short, emphatic argument I've heard against many an action or point of view. It might be a moral stand, or be as simple as wanting signs to be in the national language. The discrimination doesn't need to be explained or need a descriptive adjective. It's just discrimination.

Not only does the objector assume that discrimination is reason alone not to think or do something. So does the other person, at least when the other person is Western. The most the other person might say is, "It's not discrimination!"

When I try very hard, I remember when discrimination was a virtue. It was for centuries. Anything else lacked judgement, before judgement became a vice in the West. Discrimination flowed naturally from knowledge, reason, and loyalty. Not being discriminatory was stupid, desperate, or whorish. In the 1956 American film *Funny Face*, editor Maggie Prescott boasted that her magazine *Quality* was "the most discriminating publication in the world."

My Dutch friend Ian L, of about the same age as me, attributed the change to laws that made all discrimination seem unlawful, although only defined discriminations in certain situations became unlawful. Those discriminations and situations have become more numerous through the years. Laws passed in my lifetime prohibit us from racial, religious, and other discrimination in granting employment, making a sale, the provision of housing and other services, and so forth. We have commercial relationships, not personal ones. We don't need to meet; we have managing agents for that. We place immediate economic considerations above everything else, maximising the range of potential workers, consumers, and suppliers.

Some discrimination became illegal to ensure it became socially unacceptable. Some simply became socially unacceptable. Compelled to act without fear or favour, we mandate equality, seeing everyone the same.

So determined are we not to discriminate that in 2010, the Jobcentre Plus in Thetford, Norfolk, in England initially refused to accept an advertisement from Nicole Mamo's recruitment company seeking a *"reliable"* worker. It didn't want to discriminate against unreliable people.

In 2020, Alison Birch advertised for a hairdresser at her A.J.'s Unisex Hair Salon in Stroud, England. *"This is a busy, friendly, small salon, so only happy, friendly stylists need apply,"* said her advertisement.

Her local job centre refused to publish it. "I'm sorry," a man there explained, "but the word happy is a discriminatory word and we aren't allowed to use it, as somebody who is not happy will be discriminated against."

No longer considering ourselves peoples less than all the people on earth, our people are all people; all people are one. We're not peoples; there's nothing left to define. Ours is a single world populace, encompassing those alien to us. We're a great global unit, a universal oneness, we push further and further to a conclusion we don't contemplate. Throughout the West, our identity is trying not to have an identity.

Short of surrendering all identity and dying immediately, we can't help but discriminate. Somewhere between the thoughts deep in our heads and the atoms at the far end of the furthest galaxy, we need some point of definition. We need something to distinguish what we are from whatever we're not, in death and in life. Embracing the world doesn't end our need for identity; there remains our deepest desire for something to define us from others. We can't exist without boundaries between what each of us are and what each of us aren't, if we're not to disappear into a void of nothingness.

Wherever a person draws lines to say he or she identifies more with those within than without, there's arbitrariness. There's no end to the arbitrariness until all matter and space in the universe is exhausted. Even the division with God becomes arbitrary. Only atheists save themselves from that conundrum, for now.

To try to overcome that arbitrariness, we could have regard for what other races believe. In choosing our boundaries to define us, we could consider the beliefs that prosper and those that fail. We could reflect upon what satisfies and what doesn't. We could contemplate what's natural, respecting human nature instead of trying to change it. We could accept our innate delineations between beings.

Wanting whatever maintains and advances our qualities of life means keeping our dreams distinct from our decisions. We could remain rabid idealists for what the world can possibly be, and intelligent pragmatists for what the world really is: pragmatic idealism.

Only white people damn discrimination as intrinsically wrong; other races retain their biological relationships. Prohibiting racial discrimination in employment (in Australia since 1975) flowed from us being employers and other races applying for jobs, but other races now employ. In Sydney, Chinese employers circumvent the prohibition by advertising in Chinese.

There are sound business reasons why employers would discriminate in favour of particular races, which necessitates discrimination against others. We're open to employers employing Chinese to serve Chinese customers and so forth, although nobody imagines employing white people for white customers. We're not pandering to racists.

Employers might feel the loyalty or want the cohesion that comes from employing their own, without thoughts of other races. Workplaces are more pleasurable and efficient with senses of co-operative community, excluding anyone managers envisage disrupting the team. If workplaces are going to be tribal, with some chance of collegiality, we can't compel them to be individualistic. Prohibiting discrimination constrains people's opportunities to choose those with whom they're most comfortable, institutionalising the separations between them.

Having rejected race out of hand, we don't realise how different we are to other races. They continue unconcerned about racism, unless it's directed against them. Chinese object to prejudice against Chinese, Arabs to prejudice against Arabs. Jews object most vehemently to anti-Semitism, while recognising since the Holocaust the dangers to them that white people's prejudice represents. All the races on earth object to other people's prejudice against their own, except us.

Only white people oppose prejudice by our own. We're offended not by what people of other races say about us, but what people of our race say about others. Hungrily, we object to any hint of racism that identifies with us, likes us, and cares about us, favouring or even defending us, our histories, people, and cultures (except against other white people). We're the only race who reviles our own for being loyal to us.

Proudly without a people, our mindset is that of the world, but the world is unimaginably big. Nothing less than the whole of humanity usurps us, but humanity is too many to comprehend. Being a solitary individual becomes better than being no one at all. Ridden of everything else, we're each left alone in our mandatory isolation: individuals or everyone with no steps in between.

When other races condemn racism against their race, they assert their collective, racial identities, identifying with others from their race suffering the racism. When we condemn white people's racism, we're asserting our individualism: our separation from others among our race. We're determined not to discriminate against other races, not to be seen to discriminate, and to prevent others from our race discriminating.

Our rejection of race is a rejection of commonality and belonging. We're not to identify people, befriend them, or presume anything about them by reference to anyone else, not even thousands or millions of anyone else, and not even us. Instead, we're to treat each person as a single solitary unit. It's compulsory individualism, in our perception of others and our sense of us.

There's a painful irony in feeling like a lone voice against individualism, but we remain solitary individuals if that's all we know and that's all others let us be. The individualism we assert for ourselves we demand in each other. Ours is the triumph of individualism.

Discrimination remains. Western individualism falls away in our revulsion at white people's racism.

On the second Friday in June 1982, white man Gerry Cooney fought black man Larry Holmes for the World Boxing Council's world heavyweight championship. Don King, the fight's flamboyant black promoter, fuelled publicity around Cooney, the Great White Hope, becoming the first heavyweight boxing champion in twenty-two years who wasn't black.

Drifting out of the St James Church senior fellowship while I was drifting in was Nik, a year or so out of high school. Talking with him in the cool darkness of a winter night, Nik didn't like the racial aspects of the bout.

"I think it's just because he's a novelty," I said, wanting the white man to win. "I don't think it's any different to Arthur Ashe getting attention when most of the tennis players are white." The promoters of a New South Wales Open championship some years earlier had favoured images of black American Ashe in their posters. In spite of his successes elsewhere, Ashe lost in the first round.

Nik, an Australian, wasn't concerned about a black tennis player attracting attention. Nik wanted Cooney to lose, because he was white and his opponent was not.

When faced with a racially charged conflict involving our own, we quickly side with other races not in spite of their race, but because of it. (There was no suggestion then that races weren't real.) In a long and closely fought contest, Holmes finally prevailed.

Loyalty to our race would be racist. Our avowed disloyalty proves our opposition to racism; more divisive than race is our rejection of racism. Where there's a whiff of white racism in the air, we're eagerly against white people.

By banning racial and religious discrimination, we deny people loyalty. We also prevent any assessment of differences between races and cultures.

Blair Davies, the Taxi Council of Queensland chief executive, refused to tolerate customers complaining about the poor service of Indian taxi drivers in Brisbane in 2009. "It's racial," he said, blaming the complaints on longstanding drivers upset about losing income to Indian students. He wasn't going to defend their interests at the Indians' expense. "If you want someone to stand up for young Indians' rights to drive a cab in Brisbane, then I am happy to stand up for them."

The *Brisbane Times* newspaper report of Davies' words wasn't unusual. Later that day, I discovered the corresponding *Courier Mail* newspaper report. It mentioned longstanding Indian drivers being upset that potential passengers were passing their taxis (without saying anything) because of their bad experiences with younger Indians. The interests of older Indian drivers were reason to control who could drive taxis in Brisbane, as the interests of Australian drivers were not.

The risk of truth behind a racist perception is no excuse. It intensifies our need to reject it.

We have no sympathy for taxi drivers refusing to accept indigenous passengers, weary as those drivers are of past indigenous passengers defecating in their cabs or fleeing without paying their fares, which some drivers described to me during my years working in Redfern. They weren't saying that *all* indigenous passengers soiled cabs or ran away, and I'm sure they'd welcome into their taxis the indigenous sport stars (if they admitted sport stars at all), politicians, and professional people wearing suits. I imagine the problem passengers weren't so attired. (Politicians and professional people can be problems for reasons other than their behaviour in taxis.)

While removing the cork floor from the kitchen of our Meadowbank investment property, the second Monday in November 2020, Alex spoke of other properties being rented. When I mentioned the property having become rundown, Alex asked: "Did you have Indians renting?"

I tried to recall tenants I never met. "Yes," I answered, without certainty.

Alex told me that Indians were the worst tenants, wrecking properties they rented, compelling landlords to spend fortunes after they left to clean their properties. A man he knew refused to rent to Indians.

It was all very racist and the actions of the man Alex described were illegal, but white people cared more what other white people thought of Indians than Indians cared what white people thought of them. Alex went on to say that an Indian told him that he never looked after a property he rented. The Indian would someday buy himself a home and would take care of that home because it would be his property, but he cared nothing for other people's property.

With us leaving so much of our lives to free markets, we could let customers, suppliers, and employers (except perhaps for monopoly providers) decide whether to discriminate on whatever grounds they choose. They can decide what percentage of problem people from a particular race or religion warrants discrimination. (For white people refusing to recognise race or religious difference, one hundred percent isn't enough.) If they get it wrong, then in a competitive marketplace, they lose.

Discrimination is natural. During breaks in filming the 1968 American film *Planet of the Apes*, human actors congregated in the species of ape they'd been made up to represent: gorillas with gorillas, chimpanzees with chimpanzees, and so forth. There was no requirement for them to do so. They did so naturally.

The most profound distinction between our attitudes to animals and people is our reticence, so far, to impose ideologies of equality and inclusion upon animals. We're free to generalise about the minds and behaviours of particular species and breeds of animals as we're prevented from doing about races of people. Most often, we generalise about the capacities and temperaments of different species of dogs, the cross-breeds being the worst.

We'll contrast apes with people, as we don't contrast different races. The 2013 annual meeting of the American Association for the Advancement of Science heard Kyoto University academic Tetsuro Matsuzawa report research revealing that chimpanzee cognition mirrors, and sometimes surpasses, human capacities. He described the "extraordinary working memory" of a chimpanzee, suggesting language makes memory less essential for humans because we can transmit memory across time and space.

Harvard University researcher Victoria Wobber reported studies of African ape sanctuaries suggesting that chimpanzees and physically affectionate bonobos engage in some of the same kinds of decision making, risk management, and problem solving that people do; several studies had shown that chimpanzees recruit other chimpanzees to help them solve problems. Co-operative and cognitive differences between chimpanzees and bonobos nevertheless remained. "Bonobos may be able to better express their co-operative capacities," said Wobber, "because they are more tolerant of one another."

We examine differences between species of apes but not between races of people. The West's increasing keenness to end discrimination between humans and animals might mean we stop comparing different species of apes, or might mean we resume comparing different races of people.

With plants and animals, we vent our racial natures we can no longer express about people. Our countries exist for them.

"*Asylum seekers do not impinge on our sovereignty,*" wrote Australian senator Peter Whish-Wilson in 2014. "*But the entire world's view of whether parts of the Southern Ocean are ours depends on maintaining our presence there, not abandoning it. This decision will come at a cost and not just for the whales.*" He wanted to assert Australia's sovereignty not to curtail immigration, but to stop Japanese whaling.

The European Union is open to all races, but since 2015 not all species, pursuant to its invasive alien species regulation. After finding more than thirty American lobsters living along her west coast in the previous eight years, Sweden's environment ministry in 2016 sought to ban their live import.

With trees, we're parochial, as we find unacceptable in people. Dismissing diversity, we demand discrimination: floral discrimination, a sort of arboreal nativism, floral racism, favouring the locals. Being beautiful, elegant, and even practical are immaterial. Environmental compatibility isn't enough.

With racism came nationalism, and we've become very nationalistic with our plants and animals. Bound to plant Australian trees particularly vulnerable to breaking and falling, our devotion to indigenous trees exceeds even our devotion to indigenous people. We're willing to expunge immigrant trees.

11. TRIBES
WITHOUT RACE

"People in this community have gone out of their way to support him," said Reverend Geoff Bates of Quakers Hill Anglican Church, Sydney in November 2011, about Roger Dean. "He had an identity crisis. He would change his appearance regularly; one week he would have dark hair and the next week it would be blond."

Identity in the West is no longer about race. It's about hair dye.

No news report mentioned Dean's race, but photographs showed him to be East Asian, perhaps a Korean adoptee. I wondered whether he'd have had such an identity crisis away from the postmodern West, but Quakers Hill Anglican Church had embarked upon multicultural ministry several years earlier. Dean was also homosexual.

White people try to resolve our identity crises by identifying with others sharing our work. "The profession of nursing is deeply shocked that one of our own has been charged with murder in relation to this tragedy," said New South Wales Nurses Association general secretary Brett Holmes. Being a fellow nurse meant much to Holmes. It meant nothing to Dean.

Dean had worked as a nurse at the Quakers Hill Nursing Home, where he'd been hailed a hero for rescuing patients from a fire. We then learnt he'd set the fire to conceal thefts he'd committed. The fire had just claimed its seventh victim. It would ultimately claim eleven. Macquarie University, where Dean was one subject short of qualifying for a Law degree, had awarded him an ethics prize.

Identities we refuse about race we rush towards when talking about a profession or trade, rich and poor people, and our political bedfellows and adversaries. Work, wealth, and values became belongings by which we categorise others and ourselves, labelling people, as no other race would subscribe. They define us and own us when our races don't: our obsession with commerce and politics, now that we have nothing else. Ours are the roles employers, sellers, and elections accord us: the work that we do, things that we buy, and beliefs that we hold.

Our occupations differentiate us working bees from each other: greengrocer or taxidermist, university founder or principal. Professional associations are for education and selective representation, allying ourselves with others sharing our coincident individual interests to the extent that we do.

Among the self-esteemed occupational communities defined by our work, even lawyers speak of a legal community, but we're not communities. The most we contribute, beyond money, is answering a call up to action. From our desks, members send messages to politicians threatening our incomes. I never have.

Jobs are the tribes we leave when we change jobs or retire, or might never leave if we've nowhere to go. Our workplaces are gathering grounds; few of us take time to meet elsewhere. Without anything to unite us, employers conflict with employees, suppliers with customers.

When we don't work, we spend. "You are what you buy, lease, or drive."

Racism and nationalism once brought classes into some degree of co-operation although divisions remained, most obviously in Britain. Communism reflected classes in conflict. Without race uniting is, we've become more riddled than ever by class.

Brother Ned Gerber grew up on his family farm in Idaho. Late in the 1950s, when white America was reviewing her relationship with black America, Ned's father drove his wife and children to Ohio and the city of Cleveland. Headed home afterwards, he noticed in a car dealership window the beautiful big car he hoped to buy for his family. Ned's father parked his old truck outside the showroom, which he entered dressed in his fraying flannelette shirt, worn trousers, and boots muddied and cleaned too many times.

Ned's father was white, as were the rest of the people in the showroom, but he was a poor chicken farmer from some other place. He could afford to buy the car, with whatever sacrifice he'd need to make, but the salesmen didn't so much as speak to him. They watched him with disdain, as they might watch a stray animal nosing around, ready to speak up if it threatened to soil anything.

Only later, with his family at home, did Ned's father admit the shame that he'd felt. Salesmen who knew nothing about him but his pauper's clothes and truck dismissed him for being a hick. Those salesmen mightn't have been rich, but were richer than the father of four who'd so excitedly come to see the big car. They made the stranger feel like "a second-class citizen," in Ned's words half a century later: something less than they were, at a time they were starting to treat black Americans as equals. Ned's father never returned.

We without race define people by their clothes. "You are what you wear."

Among our friends at our parish Anglican church is a Chinese woman, married to an Australian with whom I once sat on the raffle committee. Elite private school fees for their two children kept them working; their son was a student at the school at which I'd been a boy. Jennifer was a lawyer, who around about 2010 sensed that a well-known law firm didn't hire her not because of her race or religion, but because of her ordinary handbag. The tightly groomed interviewer glanced dismissively at it during her job interview. We're comfortable with discrimination by handbag.

Rich white people dismiss poor white people, considering them stupid and lazy. Poor white people hate rich white people, considering them mean. Both think the other is greedy. Indeed, the entire Western commercial, cultural, and ideological elite and the Western masses hold each other in mutual contempt. We each think it's appropriate prejudice.

Classifying people by wealth is one thing, but in 2012, financial planner Justine Davies suggested disliking people richer than us is wealthist. She seemed less concerned about our ridicule for those poorer.

More than simply being legal, spending capacities and other manifestations of money are the premises upon which we deal with each other. "Human identity is no longer defined by what one does," said America's President Jimmy Carter the middle Sunday of July 1979, "but by what one owns."

"Everyone worth knowing has a swimming pool," my stepmother told my wife. My wife had said she and I were determined to buy a house without one.

We unabashedly congregate by our material wealth, buying homes in areas commensurate with our riches or poverty and rarely visiting the other. "You are where you live." We eat in restaurants, drink in bars, and wander shopping malls among people like us. My wife and I might yet demolish our swimming pool.

Paradoxically indeed, our individualism creates new divisions between people. *"There's a reason why Apple put the 'i' into its products,"* wrote journalist Julian Lee, of the iPod, iTouch, iPhone, and iPad in 2011, *"and it has nothing to do with information. It cannily recognised that in a world of globalised products the consumer yearned to be recognised as an 'individual'... The logo and name have become the symbol of consumerist cool, an affordable piece of luxury that, if you believe Apple's marketing, divides consumers the world over into Apple lovers and others, and ne'er the twain shall meet."* (My daughters' items I just call their i-Thingys.)

Values become so important, nobly rising above economics. Our beliefs are our identity: our ideals and convictions. Our values define us, in our Age of Ideology. "You are what you believe."

Peter Parker expressed it neatly at the end of the 2007 American film *Spider-Man 3*. "It's the choices that make us who we are," he said, "and we can always choose to do what's right."

We thus identify with people sharing our values. What we've lost in loyalty we've gained in politics: the democracy part of our liberal democracies. When we cry out for consensus and bipartisanship, we want people to agree with us. When we call for an end to division, we want them to cease disagreeing with us.

Nothing divides the postmodern West more than our passion for politics. No matter how many values we share, or presume that we do, our democratic and almost democratic elections require that we find differences to distinguish us, looking for reasons to choose. Political parties fight elections with politics.

Politics once seemed the best means of domestic salvation. It no longer does. Anyone who speaks ill of the self-serving, psychopathic, power-hungry treachery of politicians and businesspeople hasn't spent enough time with special interest groups. At least with corporations, the salaries are better.

We've allowed political conflict to pit us against each other, tearing us apart as nothing else does. While proudly developing the capacity to befriend a person without regard to race or religion, we've lost the ability to befriend people whatever their political opinions: our reasons to like or dislike them. Our passions rise for those with whom we agree, with the freedom to ostracise fools with whom we disagree. We go so far as to hate each other, even our relatives, without our same causes, or without our means of achieving those causes: who abandon our principles for others. We hate people who've never hurt us or anyone nearby.

We don't hate people from other races with whom we disagree. We respect them.

More than merely expressing opinions, we're expressing identities. Shamed by work and wealth, politics is a final identity many of us feel remains open to us.

Politically doctrinaire to one degree or another, we might enter polling booths to vote for strangers we like or we dislike a little less than we dislike others. We might say we don't care, but hate people who do. People basing their identities upon their ideals can be frightening when it's all superficial, but be more frightening when it's not.

The last Sunday in February 2013, the Republican Party was concerned about illegal immigration harming America. On his Facebook computer page, my Jewish friend Harry liked the caption, "*Keep the Immigrants: Deport the Republicans.*"

Politics means more to us than people. We might lay down our lives for the sake of a cause. Political opinions we once considered inconsequential have become reasons to be willing to kill.

In 2011, advertising company Starving Eyes released a computer game titled *Tea Party Zombies Must Die*. Participants could slaughter conservatives like former Arkansas governor Mike Huckabee and television personality Bill O'Reilly. "*The game was just a personal project*," explained agency head Jason Oda. "*I am not worried about it effecting business.*" (Advertisers presumably cared no more about his use of a noun as a verb than about murdering people for their political views.)

Politics offers tribes we can join without qualifications or conditions of entry. We believe what we believe not because it's right, but because we're members of a political tribe that believes it: conservative, liberal, progressive, socialist, whatever. We don't need to know what those labels mean, or consider the chance we're something on some issues and something else on others. More often, we decide what we are by whatever tribe is available. We believe what our mentors tell us to believe, keeping us in the tribe.

We laud our side for our intellect, selflessness, and righteousness. We condemn other sides for their stupidity, selfishness, and evil, presuming they're against us.

We do so without joining political parties. We're individuals, picking the tribespeople we meet. We concur and affirm, while nodding over coffee cups or shouting across beer.

We don't need more political parties. We need to change what we've got.

Much of the criticisms we lay upon each other is accurate, but nobody listens. Nobody's learning, too busy bickering. We don't examine our beliefs and what they imply. We don't even clarify them.

Our ideals are the identities we're not brave enough to amend; worse than being free to depart is being bound by our views. Unwilling to lose the only tribe we possess, many of us never try. Ideologies are prisons in which to be trapped.

We've greater freedom to learn when our tribes don't depend upon us keeping opinions. We might hold fast to dogmas we hold dear through our long, sheltered lives or they might develop with time, pursuing facts and reasoning that might change our attitudes. We could ruminate, argue, vote, and even reach political office, without political shades being our identities. We could debate without conflict between points of view or between means of achieving the end.

If being progressive assumes that all change is good and being conservative assumes none of it is, then we needn't be either. We could want change in one context and reject it in the next, treating each issue on its merits. We could dispense with what fails and with what once succeeded but no longer does. We can accept or reject. We could have only one class.

We used to work, spend, and opine without them being our identities. Other races still do. Work, wealth, and ideologies are our socially acceptable discriminations, not to mention swimming pools, since we ceased identifying people by race. We're people defined by features that never used to matter so much: career people, consumers, and voters. Vocational, economic, and political identities are for people without racial identities (much as they'd been under communism).

If anything is a social construct, it's money, politics, and paperwork. Careers can change, whatever our work or without it. Coinage can come to the poor and playthings be lost by the rich. We have our principles pursuing policies, but in the darkness of our minds they don't mean very much. Career politicians change their factional allegiances to serve their ambitions. Others change their beliefs, or what they say they believe, for much lesser reasons.

We can more easily move along when our identity doesn't depend upon what we or anyone else happens to do, earn, or think.

Tribes through which others and we can pass easily aren't tribes. They're variations on being individuals.

Our tribes without race are a string of descriptions we call identities, none of which mean as much as our insistence that race and religion not be among them. Descriptions aren't identities unless they define us. Multiple identities are thin films indeed, resting on nothing at all, when we need human bedrock. Identities we can change readily aren't identities. Thoughts and feelings pass. Meaningful identities don't.

Without race, we lack real identity. Other identities are superficial by comparison, no less facile than fashion. We might each be a name, and our names might be unique, but we can change our names at a whim. Losing identity is reason to place a gun to our heads, losing a description is not.

Away from the work that we do, purchases we make, or political points we score, we're alone. Without race, we have no tribes.

12. DISMISSING
OUR ELDERLY

Allocating roles to the best and most efficient providers was the traditional village model, our natural societies. They worked very well. The fittest were labour. The wisest were teachers. The able-bodied young hunted animals, gathered food, and defended the family, village, and people. The elders taught, without preventing the young from prompting innovation. We venerated the vitality and beauty of youth, knowing we once were young. We revered the wisdom and experience of age, hoping eventually to become old ourselves.

In our unnatural, postmodern West, our young still work, but ours may be the first culture in history in which they no longer listen to the elderly. Given what some of our elderly say, I can hardly blame them.

The end of our racial identities left us needing to find new identities. In place of race have arisen among us post-racial identities we imagine melding us with other races. They don't. They divide us from our own. We ended divisions with other races by creating new divisions within ours, creating new conflicts more personal and pervasive, intrinsic to our homes and neighbourhoods, than conflicts between races or religions ever were.

When World War II diminished our sense of racial connectedness, it broke down our traditional senses of authority. My father-in-law's childhood included time at the William Thompson Masonic School. In the words of a woman addressing the 2019 reunion at Cropley House, the children schooled after World War II questioned authority far more than previous children had.

Among our new Western inventions is defining people by age. Talking about his film *Back to the Future*, American screenwriter Bob Gale said teenagers came into being in the 1950s.

Our generational identities exclude us from other generations, keeping us apart. "This is my generation, baby," declared the English musical foursome the Who in the 1960s. More telling than that, the song went on to cry, "I hope I die before I get old." (I don't.)

Jewish singer Bob Dylan told Americans older than he was not to criticise what they don't understand. "Your old road is rapidly agin'. Please get out of the new one if you can't lend your hand, for the times they are a-changin'."

"Don't trust anyone over thirty," insisted Jewish campaigner for black American rights Jack Weinberg, born 1940. He and the people quoting him eventually turned thirty.

Generations are vague, much vaguer than race. Being born in 1962, I'm sometimes called the last of the baby boomer generation, born in our brief optimism after World War II. Other commentators include us among Generation X to distinguish us from Generations Y, Z, and goodness knows what comes after that.

Years of birth are artificial (they really are social constructs, as we now say about race), but we take a great deal more interest in our generation than our family or race because we think it affects us. Generations share major social, economic, and political experiences, as well as education, music, and television. (None of my children had heard of the Who, until I mentioned it.) We make informed choices, but the information changes.

Dates of birth don't change. Ages do. When we worry, we worry what will happen to us when we age rather than what happens afterwards; generations grow old together. As our postmodern West aged, discrimination according to age became unacceptable, to a point. We called it ageism, because we add the suffix "-ism" to discriminations we don't like.

Laws preventing age discrimination mean employers can't explicitly advertise for young people. They ask for someone who's dynamic.

Age isn't like other discriminations. It's one to prohibit when comparing job applicants and offering residential tenancies, but not one to wipe from our thoughts. We might employ old people, but don't have to respect them. Age is a reason to discard what somebody says.

"When a young person has to change their name because they're discriminated against," presumed Smith Family Learning for

Life team leader Anne Marmion in 2011, "it's an indication of bias and prejudice in our society and a fear of those who are different." Five out of six times Sudanese refugee Agnok Lueth applied for jobs under a false name, Daniel McClean, the potential employers invited him to sit interviews. The journalist called it Lueth's "*little white lie*," but there was no hiding his race at interviews.

Lying about his name would've been enough to rule out other job applicants, but typical was Ray of Sydney's response. "*Welcome to Australia. Unfortunately, you will find that the people at the interview (if you ever get one) will be baby-boomers – the most racist in the country.*"

Ray's generalisation may well have been true, but we don't countenance generalisations about Sudanese because they're true. We generalise no end about people from their dates of birth, we wouldn't dare generalise about them from their race or religion. Those bigotries are unacceptable, but bigotry by age is fine.

We're the worst kind of bigot, denigrating what we'll become. Among people who've forsaken much of what's natural to us, growing old is our nature from which we can't hide. If we were to think so far ahead to when we too will be old, we're so certain of the righteousness of our way of thinking, we can't imagine younger generations dismissing us antiquated fools.

They do. Without deference to our biological links, the generation maturing after World War II rejected previous generations for having made war and holocaust. It exhorted its vision of a world, but found the next generation rejecting it. We ended conservatism, as defined by former prime minister John Howard with words appearing by his wax figure at Madame Tussaud's museum in Sydney in 2013. "*A conservative is someone who does not think he is morally superior to his grandfather.*"

We call ourselves progressive because we think we represent progress, dismissing pretty well everything our silly elders think and awful forebears thought. We're happy being around other races, but not the elderly of our own.

My young children, well versed in not categorising people by their race, religion, or gender, made no end of generalisations about self-centred, thieving, and obnoxious teenagers. Each teenaged older sibling was carefully excluded from negativities, unless they were fighting. My children then became teenagers themselves.

When my eldest daughter was fourteen, she found it difficult to hate old people, even her schoolteachers. She'd also come to speak fondly for our Australian British heritage, and made me wonder how much our uniquely Western contempt for our elders mirrors our uniquely Western contempt for our race.

My Chinese friend Ted doesn't speak as we speak. He encourages young Chinese to look after their old. Never have I known a more devoted son than Ted, more devoted to each of his divorcing parents than they were to him. Chinese respect their elderly. They cherish their family and cultural traditions.

People keeping their aged parents bear children, confident those children will keep them as they age. On Ted's car registration plate were letters abbreviating his daughter's name.

Western families become commercial transactions, no less for children than parents. We live with our parents or grandparents while their cooking, cleaning, and small rent we pay make it worthwhile, estranged long before leaving their homes. Glad our parents don't try to contact us too often, we rarely think of them. Exhausting too much time close to the other is an imposition, which serves only to remind us of all we can do without them. Knowing each other by name only, we want our lives to be unrecognisable from the lives they led.

If there's a melting pot for other races in the West, then it's among them. Chau Le, an American Vietnamese lawyer in Boston, was wary of Asian men who wanted their wives to handle the cooking, child rearing, and household chores. "My dating statistics didn't look like I would end up marrying an Asian guy," she said, until the weekend she introduced her white boyfriend to her parents.

The otherwise gregarious, ambitious corporate lawyer changed whenever she entered her parents' home. "There's a switch that you flip," she explained. In her parents' presence, she was demure. She looked down when she spoke, demonstrating her respect for them. She poured them tea, sliced their fruit, and served them meals, handing them dishes with both hands. "I didn't like that he thought that was weird," she said, of her white boyfriend. "That's my role in the family. As I grew older, I realised a white guy was much less likely to understand that."

In 2010, she became engaged to Neil Vaishnav, an American-born Indian lawyer who knew not to kiss her in front of her parents or address them by their first names. "He has the same amount of respect and deference towards my family that I do," said

Le.

Ann Liu was an American Taiwanese human resources co-ordinator in San Francisco, who became increasingly uncomfortable with white men involved only with Asian women. "It's like they have an Asian fetish," she complained. "I felt like I was more like this concept. They couldn't really understand me as a person completely."

She married Stephen Arboleda, an American Filipino engineer, in 2011. They both had sprawling extended families no longer known to the West and both called older relatives Aunty and Uncle. He didn't flinch when she mentioned her parents might live with her someday.

"There are still generations of people, older people, who were born and bred and marinated in it, in that prejudice and racism," black American billionairess Oprah Winfrey told the British Broadcasting Corporation the middle Friday of November 2013, referring to elderly white people, "and they just have to die."

The respect for age that other races but ours hold dear is to their elderly own, not anyone else's. Without us respecting our elderly, nobody does. Old people are generally the nicest people around, because we all used to be nicer.

13. REJECTING
OUR YOUNG

Our generational divide isolates our young as much as our old. When footballer Sonny Quade-Folau rejected all forms of loyalty in favour of money in 2012, we didn't criticise Islanders. We criticised Generation Y, generalising about younger people's behaviour as we wouldn't generalise about races.

Following from our conflict with past generations is our conflict with future ones. The older we are, the less we want to be seen to be old (worse than age is agedness), but our obsession with youth is merely cosmetic, in the clothes we wear and colours on our faces. We've no less contempt for ages younger than ours than we have for ages older. Living so much in a moment, we forget what we said, thought, and did when we were young. We denigrate what we were.

Our ideologies of inclusion we apply to other races and religions we don't apply to children, at least not white children. Calling adults infantile, childlike, or babies is socially acceptable derision. The most striking aspect of my accountant friend Christine Fraser telling me in 1992 that I alone among her friends conversed with her five-year-old daughter wasn't that I did, but that her other friends didn't.

During a speech by Britain's Prime Minister John Major to a Conservative Party conference in the 1990s, he paused. There were many such speeches and many such pauses, but in one moment of dramatic silence, a small child cried. The audience laughed. Major smiled. It was good politics, but away from public opinion, in our cities and towns, we don't like children.

We accommodate other races as no other races do, but resent accommodating our children. Exercising our rights, we refuse.

In England in 1996, a middle-aged couple left the Spread Eagle Hotel restaurant in Midhurst, West Sussex because my family and I dared dine there on a Saturday night with young children. The woman told us that children should only eat in McDonald's hamburger restaurants.

We consider children pests. We expect to avoid them.

In Tasmania in 1997, restaurants informed us upon arrival, before we'd even thought to ask, that they offered no children's menu. Subtly, they let us know that our two small children weren't welcome. We thus weren't welcome; the only people worse than children are parents.

We'd stone to death anyone suspected of discriminating against other races, but freely ostracise our children without cause. We ban parents merely for being with them.

What had been a family home, Woolmers Estate in Longford, Tasmania had become a hotel, restaurant, and museum because the last of six generations of Thomas Archers to live there died old and childless, in the house in which he was born. The tour guide barred children from entering the house, compelling my wife and me to shifts waiting outside while the other toured.

We dread our race intruding upon us, although adults can be hard to exclude. In 2002, the Aurora residential development in Queensland catered to what it labelled the sophisticated societies like those of Europe and North America: those with pets but not children. It barred children from living there. It barred children visiting from entering communal areas without adult supervision. "You reach a stage in life where you think it's time to be selfish," said one churlish resident.

He'd reached it quickly. Aurora management would evict any woman falling pregnant.

At our local Australia Day street party in 2007, the man from number 20 was repeatedly rude to my children, the only small children there. "Are you trying to get rid of the kids?" somebody asked him.

"Well, yes," he laughed. My family and I soon left.

Later, my three eldest children slipped back to the street party trying to recover the last of the food we had brought to the party. Two much older children told my seven-year-old daughter that the party (on a public footpath and grass by the road) was by invitation only. Not only adults but older children are hostile to young children in our post-racial West.

Little wonder ours are becoming childless neighbourhoods. Few children still play in our streets; white people like it that way. We don't remark upon how few of those that do play are ours. (I best not say anything.)

The crowds at the St Ives Shopping Village on Halloween Sunday 2010 weren't much more than a normal weekend and much less than they'd become before Christmas, but children were running about. "I feel I had to complain," one fat woman with short bleached hair told the poor woman behind the counter at the centre management office, while her fat male friends leant against the counter. I couldn't help but sense she'd never complain about adults as she complained about children.

It could be hard to recall that Graham, with whom I worked at TNT and Holyman Limited, was a father and grandfather. The commercial he sent me on Good Friday, 2011 came with the caption "*Voted best commercial in Europe*," which gave me a good idea of its theme.

I was right. A screaming, fair-haired boy in a supermarket unsettled his frustrated, fair-haired father and the European shoppers looking disdainfully at both of them. A caption appeared on the screen, "*Use condoms.*"

That was Zazoo. In a 2013 commercial, the children resulting from not wearing Durex condoms wreaked years of havoc, including wrecking a sorry man's golf clubs.

The children we're most hostile towards are those that would be ours, if we identified with our race. I couldn't help but think of the furore if the advertisements featured foreign or disabled children. We discriminate against the unborn who could've been our futures, as if we'd never been children too. Perhaps we born after 1939 never were.

We assume race only ever divides people, but we've become the most divided peoples on earth: divided by work, wealth, and values, age and gender, citizenship and geography. They define and divide us because we've lost what once defined and united us. They became more important than they needed to be.

Racial belonging could breach the social, political, and economic divisions between us, the discriminations and prejudices. It does for all other races.

It's not so much racial unification, because we used to be more united than we are now. It's racial reunification. Racial reunity can overcome our differences, instead of our differences (most obviously our views about race) driving us further apart. "There is not a liberal America and a conservative America," Barack Obama told the 2004 Democratic Party convention. "There's the United States of America." We could say the same about race. Other races would, if they needed to mention it.

We fear children for being what we were, with instincts unmanaged and feelings unfettered. A notice of forthcoming seminars from the Sydney University Law School in February 2015 called the fear of young people: ephebiphobia.

Few conflicts are as damaging to a people than generational conflicts. When children feeling denigrated for being children age into adults, the only people they revile more than they revile themselves are new children coming through. We thus prevent them coming into existence: suicide Europe.

14. ANCESTRY

"You must go to where your family comes from," a Scotsman told me in Helmsdale in 1986, of my father's mother's origins on the Isle of Barra. "You must go to where your roots are."

My family name is Lennon, with the racist family motto "of an ancient Irish stock." We're best known today for the Beatle musician John, whose forebears were among many who'd long ago left Ireland for Liverpool. My father insisted that all Lennons are related, but no Beatle ever popped by our family home for a singalong. We're possibly so distantly related from John as to be closer relatives of Paul McCartney. Being British is like that, at least in Australia.

In 1998, at the edge of the town of Knocktopher in Ireland, my wife and I with our two infant children stopped at an isolated store for no other reason than the name over the door: Lennon. I wanted to buy food from the couple running the store because they shared our name, but the couple would not let me pay for the same reason.

All that united us were common ancestors we had no idea who were, but we people they'd never before met, had never before known existed, were family. We talked, feeling the affinity between us. Our kinfolk invited us to sit with them.

The family into which I was born is an amalgam of English, Scottish, and Irish, like many others in our Australian British melting pot. My wife was born to a family more Scottish and Welsh than I am.

While my accountant friend Peter and I were colleagues at Holyman Limited, I asked him about the history of his seemingly Irish family name. He shook his head in reply. "I'm just not into that sort of thing."

No longer do we count generations long dead as being us; we feel no bloodlines. I nevertheless bought Peter a key ring from a Helsinki hamburger store sharing his surname, albeit with a slightly different spelling.

Our parents, grandparents, and great-grandparents are steps along biological chains into clans, but they also reach into races. For as long as our families are racially homogenous, as families once were, they're racist. They're racist even if they're multiracial, for the races they're not. Rejecting racism makes identifying with our ancestors untenable.

We refer to race by any other term we can conjure, making vague expressions of pasts that other races call race: race without race. Every time we use words like "ancestry" and "descent" to avoid mention of race, we affirm how racist our biological links through generations are, whatever we call them. Saying "background" to mean race erodes that word as well. Without race, we're without people before us.

When I hear talk of heritage, I check myself from thinking of cultural inheritance. That is not the point we're trying to make.

When I saw a newspaper headline referring to Prince William's fiancée Kate Middleton being of mixed heritage, I assumed she was multiracial, before reading the article describe her having *"a mix of middle and working class heritage, descended from a family of solicitors and landed gentry on her father's side and butchers, plasterers, road sweepers and domestic servants on her mother's."* We'd made race akin to employment.

I'm never sure if a person's origin is the place from which the person came, was born, or whose parents or other forebears were born; a person coming from one country through another might have several origins. *"Max Morgan-Witts is a British producer, director and author of Canadian origin,"* said the *Wikipedia* encyclopaedia in 2009. Origin doesn't hark back very far, unless Morgan-Witts was an Eskimo or other Native American. Immigrants have origins upon moving countries, or upon reaching the West.

Dismissing biological linkages between people means deciding we're not born to identity, but feeling kinship with our people wherever they are can be nice for white people as it is for everyone else. Founding our identity upon race gives me something to share with a Briton in a shanty near Caracas. Losing our racial identities hasn't given me anything to share with the Koreans living across the street.

If we're not to be solitary individuals disappearing in a lonely great seethe of people, then we have to be families, clans, and races. Race is our only real means for identity: the only tangible collective identity wider than family, and we need something wider than family if our families aren't to fade away or fall in among themselves. Races are substantive, grounded in fact, set before we were born and unchanging: our forebears' shared descendants.

By race, I can live wherever I happen to live according to whatever laws governments pass, without my identity changing. I can believe what I believe, be rich or poor, change my career or politics, without my identity faltering. Whether any race produces more great composers or more serial killers than others can be matters for statisticians and analysis, but none of them need change my sense of identity. I don't become any more or less my race or family for the actions of anyone, not even me. Identities by birth endure, other identities don't.

Not as fickle as our nuclear small families passing through our fleeting little lives, our forebears offer us long families much fuller. They offer us forever.

15. FAMILY

Arabs have the proverb: "I and my brother against my cousin; I, my brother, and my cousin against the outsider."

Not us. Other races draw upon their relatives for support when conflict arises. We barely know ours.

No longer identifying with our ancestors means we no longer sense being families, beyond our nearest blood relatives we dread seeing once a year. We have only the Western notion of a nuclear family: those in the house affecting us, interacting with us or not.

We've come to regard loyalty to our families as being narrow-minded. We had to, because all the reasons why rejecting our race makes our ancestral families untenable also makes identifying with our living relatives untenable. We have no family-whole any more than a racial-whole; without racial loyalties we have no family loyalties. Relationships, such as survive, are between pairs of individuals. We've made biological descriptions of people and relationships between them incidental. Biological intimacy falls away.

Ending race ends families. We're unfettered individuals, and treat our relations accordingly. We don't just refuse to discriminate in favour of our compatriots' families. We refuse to discriminate in favour of our families. Nepotism is another discrimination we deride that other races proudly practice. Sometimes, it would be nice enough for our families not to discriminate *against* us.

After the Tiananmen Square killings in Beijing in 1989, the Chinese government praised a woman who reported a relative to the police for supporting the demonstrations. She must've been unusual for the government to promote her so eagerly, but putting politics above families has become routine in the West.

We make subjective thoughts more important than our blood relations beside us. We submit our relatives to our judgements, treating the rest of our family as we treat the rest of our race. Any familial love we feel depends upon what they think and do, although the politics we prefer aren't our people's interests. They're

96

other people's interests. Our loyalties are to other people's families.

We in the West do not simply seek to encompass the world. We are so self-serving or insecure we need to diminish the people around us. Ours is the proverb: "I and the outsider against my cousin; I, the outsider, and my cousin against my brother."

In 2008, a young American melded our rejections of race and family by publicly accusing his father of using the racial epithet: nigger. (In the West, it was newsworthy.) Only the two of them had been there when he'd allegedly used the word, it seemed, but our rejection of family leaves no leeway for a safe family home. The father objected to his son's girlfriend, although I don't know if that was because she was black. He might've not liked her anyway, and used the epithet he did to vent his feelings.

At best, we equate our families to strangers' families. (Anything else would be discriminatory.) At worst, we subordinate them.

A long-time Palestinian Arab supporter, Lauren Booth travelled with other activists by ship to Gaza in 2008 to protest against Israel's blockade of Gaza. In 2010, aged forty-three, she became a Muslim. Fifteen weeks later, in January 2011, she said her brother-in-law, former British prime minister Tony Blair, should be arrested and sent to the International Court of Justice in the Hague to be tried for war crimes for his role in the 2003 Allied invasion of Iraq. "He misled the British people and took Britain to war on a lie," she said. Booth had learnt disloyalty from her mother she'd previously called toxic and cruel.

In the parlance of our postmodern West, we don't have particular families. We have the world for that.

In our desperation to avoid war and holocaust after 1945, we constructed our grandest of all metaphors: the single world family. "*All one family so why make war?*" asks one of the tiles below the Peace Bell in Cowra.

Believing metaphors are real and whatever makes us happy, we lost ourselves in the metaphor: family without families. We without families call everyone our family; we without siblings have billions of them. Boys in Bhutan's backwaters become our brothers. Girls in Goa slums become our sisters. Therein lies our aloneness. Thinking we're related to everyone means thinking we're not related to anyone in particular.

Being Western, we're at the head of our single world family, responsible for aiding our charges; our white parents' burden.

Deeming our biological families the equals of a family in Swaziland might make us more generous to the people of Swaziland, but it leaves us neglecting our biological families. For all the Swazis' poverty and poor education, their families live for them. Ours don't. Strangers we've never met in lands we've never entered are our moral equivalent of people whose blood we share, and a possum squatting in the rafters.

Caring about all people becomes conceit by people caring for none. People trying to love everyone love no one. The result is ambivalence to the people around us. It would be nice if white people loving people cared for their families, even if that meant loving and caring about strangers a little less.

We'll call any two or more people a family even if they're unaware of each other, if they or we feel good doing so or there's money involved. Buying a Miele household appliance, or perhaps buying several, gave my wife and me the chance to join "*the exclusive Miele family*." Like our biological family, it's "*for life*."

Few of us would recall that the United Nations declared 1994 to be the International Year of the Family, with the motto "*Building the Smallest Democracy at the Heart of Society*," or be aware that the fifteenth day of May each year is the International Day of Families. Instead of helping families, we without sense of biological relationships carry out esoteric debates about what constitutes a family. We worry more about people without families feeling better than we worry about weakening family bonds.

Family would have remained a racist concept had we retained its biological definition, but ours are families without blood or other biology. They're whatever social constructs we construe them to be. "*The essence of a family is not determined by their genetic disposition*," wrote journalist Heidi Davoren in 2012, "*but rather the love that binds them*."

On that basis, we without binds have no families at all. We're individuals, like the rest of our household.

Other races still let genetic disposition determine families. Retaining their racial ethos means retaining their family ethos.

African Americans enjoy their racial identities and maternal bonds, but many fathers are absent. Part of that is due to black males killing each other and being incarcerated. That might be because Africans are so tribal, but slavery led to them losing their connection to their clans.

We recognise the damage Western individualism does to families, but only other races' families. "African Australian parents struggle to adapt to Australia's individualistic culture," said Australian parliamentarian Lindsay Tanner in his Redmond Barry Lecture of 2008, "which in their eyes sets children against their parents and undermines parental authority."

Tanner quoted the Victorian Foundation for Survivors of Torture. The "resettlement of the Dinka people from southern Sudan may mean the transition from a pastoral to an urban environment, from a communal to an individualistic culture, from a reliance on strong customary law and tribal traditions around marriage, children and family to diverse, multicultural society underpinned by values associated with individualism... The changing roles and loss of status of men, the isolation of women bringing up children alone, and the tendency of children to rapidly acquire attitudes that challenge their parents, generates tension and dysfunction within families."

Multiculturalism is individualism. Individualism is intrinsically incompatible with families. If it hadn't been for Western individualism, we'd have not let the Africans immigrate in the first place. There'd have been only European immigration.

"The ruin of a nation begins in the homes of its people," says a Ghanaian proverb. Perhaps for the West, that happened the other way around. The end of white racism appears to correlate with the breakdown of white families.

Richard R was my colleague at TNT and Holyman Limited. He was British born, his wife Joanna was also of British ancestry, but Richard liked living in what he called their multicultural street in suburban Cherrybrook, with their only child growing up without sense of race. With their nice natures and financial security, theirs was a good home, but when Richard and I caught up for dinner in Perth in 2010, they'd lost all contact with their teenage son. Richard didn't mention the race of the family with which they'd heard Jonathon was living, but mentioned it was Muslim.

Richard was an atheist, avowedly so. In spite of his and Joanna's best efforts and intentions, I wondered what belonging Jonathan found in a Muslim family that our multicultural, atheistic individualism denied him. However kind they are, parents dismissing the rest of their races and cultures are the most profound and penetrating reason for their children doing the same.

Our parents can be good people, but we whose families failed us find new senses of family where we can.

My eldest son's last primary school teacher, Mrs Smith, was a model of the postmodern West. In most respects she seemed to live by the principles she espoused, although she taught in and promoted government schools while her daughters attended an elite private school. If she had any sons, she didn't mention them.

All that distinguished Smith's daughters from other children were that they didn't call her "Mrs Smith." They didn't call her Mummy, Mum, or Mom, which might have made her seem old, and we hate seeming old. They called her by her first name.

The primary school children voted for the school captains and vice captains each year, along with three sets of house captains and vice captains. (Teachers retained an overriding veto on their choices, as guardians should.) No one explained what made a good candidate except the candidates themselves, in their short campaign speeches. "Don't just vote for your brothers and sisters," Smith instructed the children, picking out the younger siblings and any twins of candidates. "Vote for the person you think is the best candidate."

Smith espoused a world without biological loyalties, while children supported their fellow class and school students in contests with other classes and schools without adjudicating who was the best. By 2012, painted on the school playground area would be a snail holding a flag to say the school "*rocks*," along with little hearts for loving "*my school.*" We don't love our races or families, but our schools.

We don't demand other races lack family loyalty. Smith was acting school principal the last Thursday of June 2009, when two Chinese twin girls, Andra and Brigette, received merit certificates merely for being such special friends to each other.

We disavow family loyalties however good our relatives are. Other races maintain them however bad theirs are.

Hohepa Morehu-Barlow seems to have had all sorts of identity issues growing up, changing his name back and forth between the Maori form and the English, Joseph Barlow. After studying at Victoria University and claiming Maori and Tahitian royal connections, he became well known among the Brisbane elite, before police said he'd stolen sixteen million dollars from the Queensland Department of Health. "He's a naughty boy if he's done that," said his aunt Josie Boldy, "but he's still my *whanau*."

Whanau is family. Peoples identifying with their race identify with their families. Retaining their biological connections means retaining their racial and family connections.

Sitting with me in the offices of that Golden Cross Resources Limited, my former TNT Limited colleague Sarah imagined her suburban street becoming increasingly Chinese might encourage the dwindling white population to value our families, but Asians don't subscribe to some abstract ideal of families. They value particular families: their own. When they exhort families, they exhort their families, not anybody else's.

Golden Cross' receptionist was Carolyn, whose wealthy father George had felt the loneliness life could be after his wife died. The retired builder married a Chinese woman, sponsoring her and her family into Australia. When he'd established them here, through their three years of marriage, she left him, wanting more money in divorce and ultimately bankrupting him.

At the heart of our solitude is our refusal to discriminate for our relatives as other races do, commoditising them along with the rest of our commodity people. Without our families in our rampantly globalist West standing by us, nobody else has reason to do so. We don't even have reason. No one is on our side, loving us. It's the heart of our despair.

Born in 1961, Princess Diana, Princess of Wales, visited many poor and dispossessed people, sitting with potentially infectious hospice patients when few others would. "I think the biggest disease the world suffers from in this day and age," she lamented, feeling more than her fractured childhood and estranged marriage, "is the disease of people feeling unloved."

The world she described is the West. Without discrimination, there's no love. When we made discrimination to help our family seem a fault, we made loving our family a fault. We're the people unloved while our families aid other races, so proudly disloyal to their kin. Convinced we can't differentiate, we leave our relatives helpless.

Intrinsic to loyalty and allegiance is that we distinguish a person or group of people to whom we're loyal from those to whom we're not. Supporting each other has become an anathema to us.

During the Beijing Olympic Games in 2008, my eldest son asked me whether I would support him or his siblings if they represented another country. "Of course," I told him. "I'd always support any of you whoever you represented." So too would I support my friends in any contest against an Australian, although I can't imagine how one could arise. (It's only sport, after all.) Friends prevail over acquaintances I might still support, but not for being people I walk past on a footpath.

Discrimination needn't harm others. It can simply assist one's own.

Tribalism, like love and friendship, commands loyalty. Family prevails over friends, and I wonder how far my family might reach. My fond second cousin in Cirencester will never represent England in any sporting contest, unless drinking beer in his local pub becomes an event, but I'd support him against anyone, except my wife or children. Distant relatives are our clans.

If we accept discriminating for our children's benefit, we accept discriminating for our siblings, parents, grandparents, cousins, aunts, uncles, and so forth. My children's lives are worth more to me than the lives of my friends' children, which mean more to me than the lives of strangers. It thus follows my family's lives are worth more to me than other lives on earth. From being families united by blood, flesh, and bones, we become people united by blood, flesh, and bones. When identifying with our furthest relatives is morally right, so is identifying with our clan and soon enough our race, which is what scares us so much about families.

16. OUR CHILDREN

"I don't think people should have the right to kill someone who's trying to make off with their video recorder," I told my friend Peter as we debated morality, among our TNT Shipping & Development Limited colleagues enjoying a rare lunch together in a restaurant: a Thai restaurant upstairs from a Redfern Street footpath. The law said as I said, although much less eloquently.

Peter disagreed. Home entertainment wasn't so much the issue as the risk an intruder brought upon householders' lives. I'd discarded the risk for being remote, but Peter was the father of two young daughters. We were never nobler than when we abandon ideals for children we love, although it was heading out of fashion. "You just wait 'til you're a parent," he told me.

Nothing teaches us more about our parents than being parents too, leading us to sympathise with them or criticise them. Treating our children as the most important people on earth can end our last esteem for parents who didn't place us first in their lives, or even second, third, or fourth.

The day our youngest son began year one at primary school, he was in a composite class with year-two students. The second morning, he was moved into the dedicated year-one class (my wife learnt later that day) because Emma, the parent of a year-two child, complained about her son James being distracted from work by our son wanting assistance. At first I was livid for what Emma had done, before realising she'd been right. We should all be so discriminatory, supporting our children, instead of filling their heads with ideologies of inclusion and equality.

Love is discriminatory; it has to be. When we love, we discriminate.

My Chinese friend James Lee (a fellow student for a Master of Business Administration degree) said many interesting things the last time he sat in our home. A decade or so after he and his similarly Chinese wife came to our wedding, I saw him by chance in the Westfield Chatswood shopping centre. There were no end of

Chinese people in Chatswood, but James was briefly visiting Sydney from China without Irene. As was the case with so many friends, we had fallen from touch.

James brought my second son a small birthday gift. After we shared cake, we retired to the lounge room where we talked of many things, as I could with friends with whom I'd studied. James said Chinese help their children but he disparaged Western parents, who bear children but do little more than we need to raise them before casting them off.

We used to support our children, but when we read of news like the American mother of a prospective cheerleader killing the girl who kept her daughter from the troupe in the 1980s or so, we lost more faith in families. We didn't long for the senses of country, community, or other great good that made such killing inconceivable. We didn't lose faith in cheerleading.

Proudly we pursue our personal causes and careers. We condemn our children to faring alone in the world.

In her youth, British actress Vanessa Redgrave opposed American and other Western support for South Vietnam in the Vietnam War. Later, she campaigned for Palestinian Arab statehood. After the death of her daughter Natasha Richardson following a skiing accident in 2009, Redgrave recalled her daughter as a young child begging Redgrave to spend time with her. "I tried to explain that our political struggle was for her future and that of all the children of her generation," said the mother of two. "'But I need you now,' pleaded Natasha. 'I won't need you so much then'."

I never understood why Arab nationalism is so heroic a cause, but Western nationalism such a fault. Nor could I understand how Palestinian Arab statehood or Vietnam becoming completely communist helped two little English girls yearning for their mother. Redgrave cared no more, and might've cared less, for her daughters than she cared for Arabs and Vietnamese.

People of other races but ours love their families by loving their race. A Palestinian parent's love might manifest in wanting a Palestinian state. A Jewish parents' love might manifest in saying the Arabs have several states already.

We tend to think the other way around. Having rejected our racial states, our countries, we reject our families. We care nothing for our compatriots' children and are little better with our own.

Our neighbour Susan told me that having one child was "too many," drinking the wine we'd served her soon after she bought her home. Standing nearby was her teenage daughter.

Two neighbours later, beyond the locked driveway gates, a black mongrel pit bull type of dog prowled the gardened and hedge-bound front lawn. We didn't need the sign warning potential visitors: "*Forget the dog, beware of the kids!*" (While abbreviating the names of other races became offensive, we can abbreviate "children" to "kids" without anybody caring.) They often ordered their children, Saverio and Dexter, from the house. My children then played with them.

Parental individualism means our only reasons to be parents are our children's relationships with us, when we're in the mood; individualist children become individualist parents. Our care for our children is for their immediate impact upon us.

When my eldest son was in year six, parents at the years-five and six information evening cheered the teachers for making their children's annual camp as many nights as possible. No wonder my son told me his classmates aboard the bus as it was leaving also cheered.

Parents discard their children like kittens getting old. Like cats running away, children discard their parents. Who acts first is immaterial.

An Australian television commercial portrayed a middle-aged man and woman in a car watching unruly children in a car stopped near them. The couple was relieved no longer to have young children with them: relieved to be old. The commercial was, for memory, trying to sell retirement planning, but the only planning it imagined related to money rather than relationship: life without children; getting old without young people around us, provided we're financially secure.

Treating our possessions as ours alone, we refuse to imagine sharing ownership with our family any more than with our race. American Warren Buffet, one of the world's richest men, planned to give all his wealth away. "There's no reason why future generations of little Buffetts should command society just because they came from the right womb," he said in 2003, as only white people do. "Where's the justice in that?"

Where's the justice in neglecting our descendants? Rich Asians and Arabs defend not just their people's wealth but their family wealth too, building dynasties. Their future generations will command societies, because of the wombs from which they come.

The eras when we built family dynasties have passed. White people expending time away from work caring for their children can expect to be derided. Those expending their lives caring for Solomon Islands children can expect to be admired. I wonder how happy a people we might be to know our families cared so much for us, but seeing and holding our children aren't important.

In the 1999 American film *The General's Daughter*, Warrant Officer Paul Brenner investigated the death of, as the title foretold, the general's daughter. When it appeared she'd been raped, he asked Colonel Robert Moore, "What's worse than rape?"

Moore replied, "When you find that out, you'll have all the answers."

Brenner eventually found out. Worse than her rape by American Army cadets was her betrayal by her father, who'd placed ahead of his daughter his ideals: his defence of the American Army, the West Point Academy, and a thousand young men who didn't rape her. For that betrayal, not the rape, she destroyed herself. The same could be said of the West.

Through the millennia and more that ideally our families endure, the most important generation isn't the last. It's the next.

All we really know to teach our children is to learn from our failings. At this time in our histories, they should not be like us.

My wife's and my marriage created new identities for us: husband, wife, and couple. We were a union, but not a family. Our children made us a family, joining two families, as Western children once did.

I identify with my wife, because we identify with our sons and daughters. More than mere individuals, we're family because we're family to our children.

It's self-evident to say, but the only biological family of which we can be part is our own. I don't define myself in a group I don't share with my forebears, wife, and children. Any tribe to which I belong, I belong only with them.

Our family's history and future are ours; biology joins me to my forebears and children. I don't want a generational identity or any other identity I can't share with them. Caring about lives beyond our own, I care about our children and grandchildren, defending our descendants from harm.

Parenting need not be difficult, when we identify with our children. It requires loving our children and demonstrating it as best as we can. Our unconditional love teaches our children to love themselves unconditionally or would, if nothing else gets in the way. We find loving so difficult.

Looking up to us, our children make us smile, if we give them the chance. We smile because of them, if we give ourselves the chance. Like a race, we're never alone.

17. OTHER PEOPLE'S CHILDREN

The principal of our children's preschool was a lovely good-natured woman, with her sensible thick-heeled shoes and long modest dresses. Felicity cared kindly for her charges, proudly performing her job well, but had no husband or children of her own. Dithering about like a failing-minded grandmother, she could seem old before her time. Little boys and girls passed through the preschool one or two years at a time, while the only child whose image remained was one who'd never been there. She'd never been to Australia, never left her homeland, but her photograph stood on a glossy white-painted mantelpiece. She was Kamla, a young girl from the Gonds tribe in India.

Kamla's face in photograph was serious, perhaps because of an unfamiliar camera pointed towards her. She exuded more joy and pride for the school tunic and blouse she so carefully wore than all the preschool parents found in their four-wheel-drive cars crowded into the preschool parking area. Beside Kamla's photograph was a small glass jar for them to drop money to send her, as absent parents do. No doubt Kamla appreciated the generosity and amenities it brought, but she surely knew who her family was; I imagined her sharing her good fortune from the far end of the camera with her parents and two brothers. If she became the schoolteacher she said she wanted to be, she could teach us much.

Cash in glass jars and automatic debits from credit cards and bank accounts aren't parenthood. They're charity.

With Western families more metaphorical than real, there's not much of a step to metaphorical parenthood. We don't need to bear children to think we're parents, because we've made parents indistinguishable from people in positions like parenthood: *in loco parentis*. We without children or thought of bearing them call other people's children our own.

"And you're the parents?" a policeman asked a couple reporting a missing child in the 1952 British film *Hunted*.

"No," the man replied. "He's adopted."

In a flashback scene in the 1963 episode 'The Girl from Little Egypt' of the American television series *The Fugitive*, Richard Kimble wanted his childless wife Helen to adopt a child. "I won't live a lie," she told him. "I don't care if a million people lie to themselves. If I can't have a child, I won't have one!"

We understood then that parenthood was biological, nothing else, but with a long record of infertile couples adopting babies, carefully matching their race and religion. My maternal grandmother bore a child out of wedlock in 1945, offering her daughter for adoption to a childless Church of England couple in Melbourne.

Since then, we've lost interest in race and religion. We'll adopt anyone.

Adoptive parents are no longer only those unable to bear children. We might want a baby, but not want to wait the nine months of pregnancy. We might prefer the choice that comes from babies already produced to the uncertainty of speculative birth.

Our individualism doesn't confine adoptive parents to couples. "Having this wish come true is even more gratifying than I ever had imagined," said American actress Kristin Davis, living alone when she adopted a baby in 2011. "I feel so blessed." News reports spoke of her becoming a mum, quite indifferent to her merely adopting the child but for her character in the television series *Sex and the City* having also adopted a baby. At least Davis adopted her baby in America. She too had been adopted as a child.

Without biological relationship to consider, we equate adoption with parenthood, as if legal process and paperwork make a stranger somebody's child. We pretend to be parents, that other people's children are ours. "Most of us are not related by blood," said American actress Mia Farrow in 2013 of her fifteen children and adoptees, "but by love and the deepest commitment. So when we hear of children, wherever they are – when there is suffering, they are members of our family."

Farrow wasn't describing family. She was describing sympathy.

Metaphorical families have metaphorical incest. Two decades earlier, Farrow was furious when her former boyfriend, Jewish film-maker Woody Allen, became romantically involved with her adopted Korean daughter. (Thinking everyone on earth is related means all relationships are incestuous anyway, which means none of them are.) They eventually married.

Our disconnection between the reality and language of childbearing was never more glaring than in the *Sydney Morning Herald* newspaper headline, 'New 'baby' helps to heal soap star Ada's marriage.' Not watching television soap operas, I didn't know who Ada was, but I was writing this text. I imagined the quotation marks around the word *"baby"* in the headline meant that the child was adopted, but we'd gone beyond that distinction.

"We're both really happy to be in the place we are at now," said actress Ada Nicodemou, photographed smiling brightly with her husband, chef Chrys Xipolitas. His arms around her, they were both cradling her womb. "We're spending more and more time together…and we make sure we have our little date night and do things together…"

Xipolitas had been battling depression and the medication prescribed for it. "I'm not saying it's all under control," he said, "but I no longer feel I have depression and I'm not on medication. Now I talk about things…, and I really feel Ada and I are a team now."

The baby that reignited their love wasn't their flesh and blood. It wasn't flesh and blood at all. It was the Island restaurant, Sans Souci.

Outside the West, there's no talk of natural parents because the only parents are natural. There aren't birth mothers and other mothers, but only mothers or not. They have biological relationships, and not so many restaurants.

People might care for a relative's baby, but that reflects their family identity. The only children my wife and I would've offered to raise would be my orphaned nephew and niece if my youngest sister died before they reached their majority. We wouldn't have contested their grandmother acting for the sake of their well-being.

Islam allows fostering of children, but bans adoption outright, safeguarding patrimony and inheritance. Egypt extended the ban to Christians, for fear they might adopt Muslim babies and raise them as Christian. In 2009, Egypt prosecuted American citizen Louis Andros, his wife Iris Botros, a dual Egyptian citizen, and an American couple for adopting babies in Egypt.

Nowhere does our Western witlessness about race meet so spectacularly with our paternalistic and maternalistic attitudes to other races than in the practice of childless white people flying across the world, traversing every biological and cultural schism, to bring home what we think are commodity children. Ending our biological link through generations, we don't simply end our family lines. We replace them with other family lines.

We're not alleviating population pressures in the countries from which we adopt. With two children already, the singer known as Madonna (born Madonna Louise Veronica Ciccone) adopted Yohane Banda's thirteen-month-old son David from Malawi to take home to Europe. Banda sired another child to replace him.

Foreigners, eighty percent of them American, adopted fifty thousand Chinese babies in the ten years to 2006, before the Chinese government insisted that adopters be in stable marriages, have sound finances, and not be overweight. When an earthquake killed seventy thousand people and destroyed seven thousand schools in Sichuan province in May 2008, overseas offers weren't just of aid. Overseas adoption organisations rushed to inquire. Chinese people also offered to adopt orphans, but they were only ever going to adopt Chinese babies.

Our global adopters might be eager and even emotionally desperate to be parents. They might want to help the poor children, presuming they're as oblivious to race as we are. They might want a plaything, toy, or pet human in the house.

Whatever the motivation, I imagine few adopters wilfully mistreat their adoptees. Most ply them with material wealth and something like love, much as white Australians from 1909 until the 1970s treated mixed-race and other Aboriginal children whose indigenous parents were unable or unwilling to raise them. At the very least, we thought we could parent them better than their parents could. Governments removed those children from their people and entrusted them to white foster parents.

Among the government officials removing those babies was a board member of the Royal Queensland Bush Children's Health Scheme and its field superintendent for North West Queensland. "I didn't care whether they were Protestant, Catholic, or Calathumpian, or whether they were black, white, or brindle," he later told his grandson, much later a friend of mine. "If a child was in danger I had to take it. I took children from white farmers, I took kids from Italian sharecroppers, but I took kids from more Aboriginal families because more of their kids were in danger." He explained that the danger came primarily from male Aborigines, especially when intoxicated.

Late in the twentieth and early in the twenty-first century, the West's romantic visions of other races and cultures and our hostility to our own can't imagine such a past (or present). Our only explanation for removing black babies from their communities is the genocide we're certain our forebears pursued.

So quick to malign our forebears, we presume that white parents, homes, and education harmed those indigenous children. Cleverly able to coin a new phrase, we have come to call those children the stolen generations, but there was no stolen generation. They were saved generations: generations of Aboriginal children, along with other children, saved from danger and neglect by well-meaning officials and the foster parents who cared for those children.

The so-called stolen generations were the subject of several white Australian sorry days, beginning the last Tuesday of May 1998. On the second Wednesday of February 2008, the Australian prime minister led a national apology, with audiences gathered before huge television screens in public places. Schools adjourned their classes to watch it on television, much as schools in my childhood adjourned classes to watch America land two men on the moon.

"Prime Minister Kevin Rudd's apology to the Stolen Generations, for past government actions and policies of separation steeped in racism," wrote journalist Virginia Haussegger afterwards, *"was a sobering reflection on our history. For some of us it was an awakening: a moment of new understanding. It was as if a deep cultural fault line had shifted."*

Liberal Party leader Brendan Nelson rose to endorse the apology, but made the mistake of mentioning the context in which we'd removed the mixed-race children from Aborigines. *"Without warning,"* as Haussegger described it, *"smashed-up images of Aboriginal rapes and little girls being drowned and petrol-sniffing teenage criminals and drunken Aboriginal men sexually abusing babies were flung out at the audience."*

All we wanted to hear were evils of our wretched past: not our forebears trying earnestly to help. We heckled and jeered. Some rose and turned their backs on Nelson. We should have left the Aboriginal children in filth with their people around.

"Had he forgotten the Aboriginal elders present," asked Haussegger, *"the sons, the daughters, the broken families, many who'd travelled many*

kilometres, and waited years for this day? Of course no society can excuse the inexcusable. But at this moment Nelson's timing was way off, his insensitivity breath taking."

We had no sensitivities for our retired government officials and foster parents we so widely maligned, many of whom were still alive. We complained about Nelson's timing, but there never is a time in which to talk of our forebears trying to be kind and their racism having reason. I never again heard of someone so publicly mentioning it.

Nelson was also my local parliamentarian. More than ten years earlier, he was a backbencher humbly addressing a group of residents newly moved into his electorate, squeezed into the atrium of a modern office building in Lindfield. Speaking of the squalor and neglect in which many Aboriginal children still lived, his desire to help them was palpable.

Among the people claiming to have been stolen was Aboriginal activist Charles Perkins. He said the offer an Anglican priest, Father Percy Smith, made to his mother Hetti to take him at the age of ten to an Anglican hostel for boys in Adelaide "was an offer my mother couldn't refuse." It is hard to believe he would later become the first Aboriginal male to be awarded a university degree, in 1966, without it.

Our apology came to mind when I saw two white women among our group at the Glenrowan Tourist Centre, the first Friday of 2013. They each wore wedding bands, and one stroked a full-blood young Aboriginal boy as if he were her son. The details of the process by which she came to stroke him had changed from the process we now call stealing a generation, but the result was the same. If our mood for apology continues, we could have a lot for which to apologise there.

On the third Thursday of March 2013, Prime Minister Julia Gillard formally apologised to those affected by Australian governments, churches, and social workers pressuring a hundred and fifty thousand white mothers to give up their babies for adoption from the 1940s to the early 1970s because they were unwed, although that apology came with none of the fanfare of apologising to Aborigines. The rest of us barely noticed. We didn't join in.

Liberal Party leader Tony Abbott did. He infuriated adoptees and their mothers by speaking of "birth mothers" instead of simply "mothers." He thus apologised for his previous apology.

Britons, New Zealanders, Americans, and Canadians did the same through that period. Americans now call theirs the Baby Scoop Era.

We're still scooping other people's children. Academics from nine Australian universities wrote to the government's Forced Adoptions Apology Reference Group in 2012, referring to growing research that the "*loss and pain*" suffered by overseas mothers "*is at least equal to that of mothers in Australia.*" The dean of graduate research at the Royal Melbourne Institute of Technology, Denise Cuthbert, said international studies showed birth mothers were often separated from their children because they were single, widowed, divorced, or poor.

The circumstances of foreign children today are normally much cleaner and safer than were the Aboriginal missions half a century ago but, if removing those Aboriginal children was so harmful to them, the removal of foreign children today must be more damaging. Korean HeeRa Heaser was among the international adoptees signing a letter in 2012 claiming to "*have also suffered similar hardships...including displaced belonging, disempowerment in relation to access to adoption information and their identity, and a profound sense of loss.*" She cited a 2005 government committee report pointing out that international adoption came at the expense of domestic adoption.

The world's oldest international adoption programme is in South Korea, where a 2009 survey found only homosexuals were more shunned than unwed mothers. "Most of the Korean adoptees I know have confronted problems in the search for their family," said Kim Myung-Soo in 2012, "half records, false information, whole files missing." Until her late twenties, she believed she'd been born out of wedlock to Korean factory workers, before learning that Koreans forced her mother to give her up for adoption after her father died. She too wanted an apology for being adopted by an Australian couple when she was four years old, believing international and domestic adoption should each have a separate apology. "Including inter-country adoption is not going to reflect the complexities of two different cultures, two different historical contexts and two different lived experiences."

In October 2012, a Korean twenty-four years old from Sydney filed a complaint with the attorney general upon learning she'd been unlawfully adopted; a midwife had told her unwed mother she'd been stillborn. With many international adoptions lacking freely given consent but involving deception and coercion, adoptee support groups complained that Australian governments failed to prevent overseas children being removed in conditions it opposed in Australia.

In her 2013 book *The Child Catchers: Rescue, Trafficking and the New Gospel of Adoption*, American journalist Kathryn Joyce described the continuing practice of babies in countries like Vietnam being wrenched from their mothers to fuel overseas adoption. An American family was told the two Ethiopian sisters they were adopting were orphans living in destitution after their parents died from the human immunodeficiency virus. In fact, the girls' father was alive, uninfected, and told he was sending his daughters to America for their education.

"It is a way for churches to get involved in poverty and social justice issues that they had ceded years before to liberal denominations," wrote Joyce, *"an extension of pro-life politics, and a decisive rebuttal to the taunt that Christians should adopt all those extra children they want women to have."* She called it a *"saviour complex."*

Joyce acknowledged the good intentions of many adoptive parents, but all the problems of the past remain. "I don't feel like we were adopted," said CeCe, one of six Liberian orphans adopted by the Allison couple in Tennessee. "We were sold."

There may well come a time we conduct sorry days all round the world, apologising for having adopted foreign children. Aged adopter parents might remark they acted with the best of intentions and government approval, but no one will listen. Anyone mentioning the fine lives they afforded the children they treated as their own or the harsh lives the children left behind can expect to be jeered. Nothing will diminish our descendants condemning us, before they prostrate themselves in shame.

18. OTHER PEOPLE'S FUTURES

For thousands of years, Badolato repelled invaders from her hilltop fortress, before the birth rate among Italians became so low around the new millennium 2000 that towns like Badolato welcomed Kurds bringing children. We applauded the Kurds' arrival for keeping the beautiful town vibrant and alive, as if people are interchangeable. We deem Badolato an Italian town purely for its stones and mortar being in Italy, but the Italian men and women were old, while Kurdish children played. Badolato was becoming a Kurdish town.

Other peoples but us continue identifying as human beings distinct from other animals and as races distinct from other races; we don't begrudge them their racial, special, and familial identities. They recognise biological links between people in family and race, seeing boundaries around their clans and traditional tribes. They feel their families. They revel in race. Their shared ancestries quietly bring them together. Some find lesser boundaries around their religion. They value themselves: their peoples and cultures. Those people so assured in their race are growing.

If they're not growing, they're keeping their countries to replenish someday. They're emigrating, without disappearing at the rates we are. The peoples of the world persevere.

Every twelve years, Chinese birth rates boom for it being Years of the Dragon, not only in China. An additional two thousand seven hundred babies were born each day in 2012 in China alone. Sales of nappies rose seventeen percent.

Sales weren't the reason Taiwan wanted its people to have more babies that year, as I learnt from a radio report on the Lunar New Year enthusing about Australia becoming Asian. Also welcoming the baby boom was Hong Kong, where births rose five percent in 2000, the last Year of the Dragon. In Singapore, they rose ten percent.

Not only was the Singaporean government concerned about the

country's low birth rate. Mint-manufacturer Mentos released a three-minute advertisement on Singapore's National Day 2012 encouraging Singaporeans to bear children: to conceive them that night. "It's time to do our civic duty," said the short film to music. "I'm talking about making a baby."

The motto for Singapore's national day was "Loving Singapore, Our Home." (Australian national days focus upon welcoming immigrants.)

Japanese governments, companies, and people don't respond to their low birth rates with talk of immigration, except of ethnic Japanese. In 2014, the Japanese government began funding matchmaking services, consultations, and marriage information. (There are none of the catalogues of foreign brides-to-be that white people peruse.) Prefectural governments could apply for grants of up to forty million yen for new projects to support marriage, pregnancy, birth, and child rearing. Childless couples don't adopt foreign children.

While rich white people adopt Korean babies, Korea is also suffering a low birth rate. In 2010, the South Korean health ministry was charged with trying to increase the numbers of Korean children (but not to satisfy Western demands for adoption). To "help staff get dedicated to childbirth and upbringing," it switched off the lights in its offices once a month. "Going home early may have no direct link to having more kids," said Choi Jin-Sun, in charge of the project at the ministry, "but you cannot just completely rule out a possible link between them." Among the measures to increase the birth rate, the ministry paid parents cash.

While Western companies increase working hours to increase productivity, Koreans look further ahead. In June of that year, the Economic and Social Development Commission encouraged its labour force to work less to find time to make babies, create jobs, and boost productivity. Backed by the South Korean government, it planned to cut average annual work hours to less than nineteen hundred by the year 2020. It sought to change the wage system to factor in productivity and discourage longer hours. "Long work hours result in low productivity, undermine job creation, and contribute to a low birth rate," said spokesman Kim Yang-Soo, "thus acting like a stumbling block to the country's development."

The commission also encouraged job sharing and flexible work hours to create jobs, while saying employees should no longer be able to purchase unused holidays. They should be compelled to use them. "Female workers, for example, avoid getting married and having babies because of work burdens. Use of more part-timers to stand in for them would allow them more time for managing homes and caring for babies."

Lee Jeong-Ho, a policymaker at the militant Korean Confederation of Trade Unions, wanted the government to use tax incentives to encourage companies to reduce work hours. The basic wage of employees at large manufacturing companies accounted for only thirty percent of their income, pressuring them to work overtime.

Local governments in Korea also ran schemes to increase the birth rate, such as providing matchmaking services. The Gangnam district of Seoul, with one of the lowest birth rates in South Korea, arranged mass blind dates among its residents. It paid couples one million won to bear a second child, five million to bear a third, and ten million for a fourth.

There are no such campaigns in the West. Our councils worry about trees.

The fates we care about aren't ours. With more than a million members in 2014, possibly the largest club in Britain (other than those providing services to members such as automobile clubs and trade unions) is the Royal Society for the Protection of Birds. From our emptying homes, we write letters to large dictators in small African countries trying to save endangered species such as the rufous fishing-owl. We never feel nobler than we feel finding a little time to save something.

We don't finish one campaign to save the world before taking up the next, but if we really wanted to save the world, we'd save our corners of it. We'd save ourselves.

If Britons and other Europeans were species of badgers dwindling away, we'd be writing letters, giving money, and marching in the streets campaigning to preserve our people: preserve us. Were a tribe of Amazonian Indians dying without enough of them being born, we'd be falling over ourselves to protect them. Unwilling to save ourselves, we're saving everyone else: other people's families, everyone but us.

To care about a people dying, we don't have to like each other. We needn't love those who don't love themselves. Caring that

Swedes, Slovakians, and Slovenians survive and prosper is like caring that human beings survive and prosper, particularly for a Swede, Slovakian, or Slovenian. It's like caring that our clans and families survive. If we don't care about our flesh, blood, and selves, nobody will, beyond the point of our decease.

If the first step to changing things is identifying them, then talking (or writing) about them is just a second step. What might come to matter is the third.

With the population of central and northern Spain depleting, Spaniards set up Asocamu in 1995 to promote the repopulation of some of the country's picturesque villages. With up to a hundred of the five thousand villages faced abandonment by 2012, it organised a bus tour for sixty-eight hopeful women from Madrid to Candeleda, a town five thousand years old.

It wasn't much. Candeleda isn't confined to Spaniards, with almost a hundred Romanians then living there.

In February 2012, American Health and Human Services secretary Kathleen Sebelius told the House of Representatives Energy and Commerce Subcommittee on Health that health insurers paying for contraception would improve their profits because they avoided the costs of pregnancies. "Family planning is a critical health benefit in this country," she said, "according to the Institute of Medicine."

Everything's economic in the West: the economics of individuals. Only individuals consume. Parenthood is consumption and parents are the consumers: not the children, family, or people. Children without money aren't consumers.

Seeking votes as much as fearing a future dearth of workers, spenders, and taxpayers, the Australian government began paying money to people becoming parents late in the 1990s, but didn't discriminate between parents and those taking other people's children. That might've meant the same Korean child could attract a Korean government payment at birth and Australian government payments upon adoption. The Australian government ceased payments in 2013.

Financial benefits we pay parents without discrimination are another beacon for immigrants. We used to argue their improved standards of living in our countries reduced their birth rates to less than they would have been in theirs, before deciding we want them here to propagate. Basel, who installed our second alarm system at home, was an Iraqi, who told me that New Zealand officials preferred families among the people they brought to their country. (He later moved to Australia.)

Western interests are immediate; we don't want to wait. Businesses trading in baby products are as impatient as others to make a quick sale. Immigrants with families already in place and adoptions bring new generations into the fold much sooner than waiting nine or more months for pregnancies to bear customers.

We're no longer people or nations. We're markets.

Unless we're selling disposable nappies and brand-name baby clothes (adding to costs people perceive in becoming parents), we'd rather advertise our product than parenthood. A glass-topped coffee table is easier to buy than a baby easily born, and easier to discard. If we marketed parenthood as well as we market products for sale, then we'd all want to be mothers and fathers.

Esoteric masses of indeterminate people willing to buy or sell we call markets. Our glorious markets for purchase are all over the place: in homes and factories, schools and offices. Every point of our lives, through our work, shopping, and sleep, we're members of thousands or more markets: one for toothpicks, another for aeroplane seats. We're markets for socks we should probably buy and shoe shines we might possibly want. We can be bald but be in the market to buy hairbrushes or frilly nightwear, for the chance we buy one for a gift.

We speak of markets much as other races speak of societies, with interests, objectives, and knowledge. They presume their people to be valuable and great much as our forebears spoke, presuming to speak for us. We feel the same about markets.

We needn't feel those markets to be in them, remaining when we've finally bought. The only way to escape markets for good is dying. Becoming insane or comatose isn't enough.

We're bequeathing our lands to others. "Shortly, fifty percent of the American population – less than fifty percent – will be of European stock," said American vice president Joe Biden during his speech to Sichuan University in Chengdu, China, the third Sunday in August, 2011. Among people determined not to be racist, "stock" is another of those words that mean race.

Instead of our diminution making us think we're doing something wrong, it makes us more certain how wonderful we've become. "So we are the most – we are an incredibly heterogeneous nation," continued Biden. "That's part of our strength, that's part of the boundless capacity of the American people, but it's also because of the enduring strength of our political and economic system and the way we educate our children, a system that welcomes immigrants from across the globe who enrich our national fabric and revitalise our diverse multi-ethnic society."

We're smitten with our self-destruction, never so proud of being a people as we're proud of not being one. Biden's comments followed the 2010 American census, which found for the first time that white babies were a minority of babies born in America. By 2014, white Americans were a minority of children under five years of age. More white Americans are dying than being born. White Americans will be a minority by 2043.

Confusing populations with people, we rarely talk about our dearth of babies. It's no longer news, except to Biden.

Such forecasts had been around at least since 2008. "Rather than being resistant to it," said Martin Cantor, the director of Dowling College's Long Island Economic and Social Policy Institute in New York, in 2008, "we have to make it work as smoothly as possible so the economy and the social fabric benefits." Whatever social fabric meant if not society, Cantor was confident racial tensions could be managed.

Aside from gloating over the passing of our people, our only other responses are economic. "It's critical that children are able to grow to compete internationally and keep state economies rolling," said Laura Speer, co-ordinator of the Kids Count project for the Annie E. Casey Foundation in Baltimore in 2010.

William Frey, a Brookings Institution demographer who analysed the 2010 data, said "the new census, which will show a minority majority of our youngest Americans, makes plain that our future labour force is absolutely dependent on our ability to integrate and educate a new diverse child population."

Immersed in our world of data and lists, all that matters is an artificial construct of numbers called an economy, not a people, civilisation, or quality of life. We proudly reduce people to their contributions to commerce: their work and trade. Human populations matter by their economic impact upon us. It's all we perceive.

In such an environment, dinner-party conversations become rote. Asking someone "What do you do?" becomes a euphemism for "How much do you earn?" and "Can I buy something from you, sell something to you, or hire you?" In cities like Sydney, the question soon following is "Where do you live?" It's a polite way to ask, "How much can you afford to pay?" and "Is it worth my time travelling to sell something to you or to buy something from you, or worth your time travelling for me to hire you?"

We're uncompromising commercialists, driving ourselves to extinction. Even Tony Perkins, president of the Family Research Council in Washington, emphasised the economic impacts of minority races becoming America's majority; single-parent families are the most dependent on government assistance. "The decline of the traditional family will have to correct itself if we are to continue as a society," he said in 2010, as if America were still a society. "We don't need another dose of big government, but a new Hippocratic oath of 'do no harm' that doesn't interfere with family formation or seek to redefine family."

From a distance, people are dollars and cents. Close by, they're ladders towards and hurdles obstructing what else we want. Our people can die without our deaths appearing in the national accounts.

It's much the same story throughout our postmodern West, trying to keep up with America. Europeans will be a minority in Great Britain before 2100, although the demographer forecasting it wanted to remain anonymous for fear of being called racist. Much sooner than that, cities like Leicester will have what are politely called plural populations by 2019. The forecaster identified thirty-five British cities where white people will be the minority by 2037. The West without race leads to a world without the West.

There's been little reporting of these forecasts and no public discussion about them. I saw or heard no comment about Biden's remark, which I discovered only when I read a transcript of his speech. Because it's us, no one talks about it. If demographers in other Western countries are making racially based population projections, they're unwilling or too fearful to publish them. If only they were as proud of our demise as was Biden, they could sing it from the rooftops.

19. RELATIONSHIP
AND MARRIAGE

The Rich Task Presentation Supper for my eldest daughter's year-eight high school class was interesting not just for the relatively wealthy children from relatively small families talking tirelessly about world poverty and overpopulation. My daughter mentioned them because, she later explained, "it sounded good."

Without bloodline or other biology to define us, the West perceives populations oblivious to heredity. "Mexicans didn't speak Spanish before the Spaniards came," said one girl, failing to distinguish Aztecs and other American Indians from Spaniards and even that portion of the Americas from what became Mexico. She wasn't assuming that only Aztecs were Mexicans. She had the same abstract vision of Australia. "We didn't speak English before the English came," she said. She wasn't Aboriginal.

Conversely, children and adults alike spoke of Europeans as if we weren't. We are where we live. The Asians didn't make the same mistake about Asia, although the few of them there that night said little.

Our postmodern West plays havoc with natural human instincts, but studies have shown we still instinctively tend to choose spouses that look at least a little like us. Popular folklore holds that men marry women like their mothers and women choose men like their fathers. My law school girlfriend, sometime through or past the end of our relationship, told me I should marry someone like my mother. Whether or not I said as much, I thought she'd marry someone like her father. Our natural instinct is to mate with our own.

In 1883, the American Supreme Court decision of *Pace v Alabama* upheld that state's anti-miscegenation law. By World War II, thirty-eight American states banned interracial marriage involving white people. Marrying within our race requires an air of racism much like the air of speciesism in not marrying chimpanzees, fish, or pot plants.

SIMON LENNON

The Fourteenth Amendment to the American Constitution, adopted in 1868, granted Negroes citizenship after the Civil War. The Jewish Holocaust led to judges interpreting it way beyond anything previously imagined. In the 1948 case of *Perez v Lippold* (known also as *Perez v Sharp*), the Californian Supreme Court overturned that state's anti-miscegenation laws as a breach of the Fourteenth Amendment. In the 1967 case of *Loving v Virginia*, the American Supreme Court overruled *Pace v Alabama* altogether, overturning America's remaining anti-miscegenation laws.

Interracial relationships weren't yet compulsory; there are no legal prohibitions on us choosing our friends, lovers, and spouses by race (even if some people sleep with whomever they can). Based upon his 1958 novel, Englishman Graham Greene's 1959 screenplay *Our Man in Havana* centred upon Britain's Secret Intelligence Service operative in Cuba, James Wormold. His wishes for his beloved daughter living a happy life included her marrying a fellow Anglo-Saxon.

Other races still think as much. Adrienne was a pretty Jewess I counted among my friends studying economics at the University of New South Wales, late in the 1980s. She'd never seemed religious, but in a cafeteria enclave in the Sydney central business district to which I'd invited her one day, she spoke of marrying a Jew in such a tone to mean she wasn't becoming romantically involved with me. I don't think she was letting me down gently.

The 1993 American film *The Pelican Brief* starred white actress Julia Roberts and black actor Denzel Washington. In the book upon which the film was based, their characters became romantically involved. Roberts was quite happy to repeat the romance in the film, but Washington thought his black female fans would be upset to see him kissing a white woman.

"I don't see colour," claimed Aboriginal Olympian and senator Nova Peris in March 2014 of her current husband Scott Appleton. "I see the man I love."

It wasn't true. Peris' previous husband Daniel Batman, the father of two of her children, was also white. While married to him, Peris sent Trinidadian athlete Ato Boldon a photograph of herself naked. *"Its hard to keep a good woman down, and a black woman like me at that..!!"* she wrote to Boldon on the middle Wednesday of March, 2010. *"White men can't control black women they think they can but can't."* Her reason for marrying white men wasn't white men but black men. "*If I was to marry a black man here u have to marry the family lol...and that is just too much, I am the eldest of 45 cousins...on my side imagine family reunions lol...*"

Her private correspondence was a world away from the rejection of race she spoke publicly. "*I don't want to say...I wish I had...Ato when he came to Australia,*" she told Bolton, "*cause I regret that I didn't 10 years ago, wish I wasn't the reserved person I was back then the shy girl...lol...so my dear friend I am waiting for you...finally BLACK...just like a Tim-tam...black on black xxx.*" Tim Tams were double-layered brown chocolate biscuits.

While interracial marriage rates were rising for other races in America, they were falling for Asians because immigration gave them more opportunities to marry within their races, although their rate was still among the highest of races. Boston-born Liane Young, an assistant professor of psychology at Boston College, hadn't thought twice about interracial relationships when studying philosophy at Harvard University, but went onto marry Xin Gao from Fujian province in China. "We want Chinese culture to be a part of our lives and our kids' lives," she said in 2012, saying a racially homogenous marriage felt right. "It's another part of our marriage that we're excited to tackle together."

A sense of family stretching beyond their living room walls into their ancestries led them to marry within their race. They shared a common culture, heritage, and future with each other and their children.

Not so white people. Responding to the results of a 2009 survey by the Victorian Health Promotion Foundation (called, as we might call an old friend, Vic Health), Emily Howie, the director of advocacy and strategic litigation at the Human Rights Law Resource Centre in Melbourne, insisted multiculturalism "*must be deeper than dumplings in Chinatown followed by gelati in Lygon Street.*" Any hint of our past racial loyalties is too much.

We must hold particular beliefs about race, whatever the facts or our experiences, but thirty-seven percent of respondents felt people of different ethnic origins "*sticking to their old ways*" weakened Australia. We're supposed to think that immigrants retaining their cultures somehow strengthen us; anything else would be our loss. Thirty-six percent said some groups of people (Muslims, Middle Easterners, and Asians being most commonly cited) didn't fit within Australian society, but we have to believe they all do (even while sticking to their old ways).

Howie was most concerned that "*nearly one in ten of us do not believe that people of all races are equal or that inter-racial marriage should be supported.*" (I don't know whether "*us*" was all Victorians or just the white ones.) A figure of one in ten might seem small, but one in ten million would've been too many. Interracial marriages aren't simply to be tolerated but supported. We need not just to welcome other races into our neighbourhoods but to marry them. Merely living together isn't enough.

"*On the whole*," wrote Howie, "*Australia might be a tolerant, open-minded society that is supportive of multiculturalism... But is near enough good enough?*" Much like an alcoholic beginning the path to recovery (rather than one who takes a nibble of Scotch on her birthday), Howie invited gestures reputedly like those at meetings of Alcoholics Anonymous. "*They say the first step towards recovery is admitting you have a problem. Well, let's say it like it is. Racism exists in Australia.*" This was Racists Anonymous.

Not content with such cleansing, Howie went onto own other white people's racism: a collective, tribal sense not so much of our race but our racism and revulsion towards it. "*We hear it, some of us practise it and many of us tacitly condone it. The time has come, in our individual and collective actions and attitudes, including those of our leaders, to acknowledge and denounce it, so that we can move forward.*"

We're not moving forward. On the one hand, we espouse a world without race. On the other, we dispense with pretence when it's a chance to prove we're not racist, not anymore.

Race was central to what journalist Heidi Davoren in 2012 called "*a liberating discussion on mixed-race unions that I hoped was more the norm than the exception.*"

"I prefer to date white women," said an Asian male.

"I prefer to date Asian women," said a white male.

"I prefer to date black men," said a white female.

Apparently, preferring to date other races isn't racist. Preferring to date our own is, although it's hardly prejudiced against other races (and might be doing them a favour). We no longer allow the similarities with us we desire in our spouses to include race.

In May 1995, Prince Joachim, the second-born prince in the Danish Royal Family, announced his engagement to Alexandra Manley, a Eurasian born in Hong Kong. My Jewish friend Ian Biner (who'd spent considerable time in Denmark investigating and establishing a ferry service for Holyman Limited) told me there wasn't even a ripple of comment about her race within Denmark. Danish people's indifference to their new princess' race proved, said Ian excitedly, how far Europe had come from her racial past.

A couple of months before Joachim's wedding, I dined with the chief accountant of our new Danish subsidiary company in a beer hall in Aarhus. Bent (who'd surely spent time with Ian) told me Danes were very upset their prince wasn't marrying a Dane or even a European.

After bearing two Eurasian sons, the couple divorced. Joachim didn't let the failure of one marriage ruin his view about marriage, although it might've affected his view about interracial marriage. He learnt and moved onward, marrying a Frenchwoman, Marie Cavallier. They have two children and are still married.

If we don't value ourselves there's no reason others will, except that some others do. Talking with me in the lounge room of my home, my Chinese friend James Lee thought a future generation of Chinese men wouldn't mind if the Chinese preference for sons over daughters led to a shortfall of Chinese women. They'll take Western women. It was strictly a last resort, for the lonely excesses of men unable to secure Chinese wives. James didn't speak of Chinese men taking women of other races, but might've known white people were most amenable to interracial marriage. Nor did he mention my young daughters.

Jane Duncan Owen's 2002 book *Mixed Matches: Interracial Marriages in Australia* spoke of the problems of mixed-race marriage being much like those of multiculturalism, which journalist Katherine Feeney also acknowledged in her newspaper article referring to the book. Striving to overcome both, we're unwilling to investigate whether interracial marriages are more likely to fail than marriages within a race, unless we can argue they're not.

The interracial marriages I've observed most likely to survive (like the racially homogenous marriages I've observed most likely to survive) are those grounded in a common, devout religion. With or without that commonality, we do all sorts of crazy things from emotional desperation or, worse than that, what we think is love.

At Otter Gold Mines Limited, Sharon was more fun than I'd have expected a chief accountant to be. When she wasn't good-natured, she enjoyed it, except when she complained about the former legal general manager bringing his children into the office during school holidays. Being around thirty years old, overweight Sharon joked unconvincingly about never getting married in spite, or perhaps because, of her career. (The people unhappiest about something laugh loudest about it.)

At the end of one working day, Sharon shared the taxi I boarded across the Harbour Bridge to Martin Place with a driver recently arrived in Australia, as were most taxi drivers in Sydney. His knowledge of English was poor, but enough for me to stagger a simple conversation with him beside me while Sharon sat behind us. The short journey lasted five or so minutes before I departed, paying for the full journey to take Sharon the short distance along George Street to Central Railway Station, for memory.

"He was just waiting for you to go," Sharon told me on Monday, "so he could tell me about his friend." He told Sharon he thought she would like his friend and she gave him her telephone number. (I hope it was only her work number.)

Never was Sharon's loneliness more evident. A longer trip I could've understood, but not the few minutes that evening.

Sharon insisted she was only meeting the driver's friend in a bar. He proved to be a jet-black Nigerian, whose visa allowing him to remain in Australia would shortly expire. Their relationship, if that's what it was, quickly flourished, with her raving about how nice he was and how well they related together. She called him her boyfriend, paying for whatever he wanted. Sharon was pleased that people in Sydney didn't flinch seeing a white woman with a black man, as they'd flinched when she took him to Brisbane.

"People in Sydney," I explained, "are much too self-absorbed to notice *anyone*."

"Once you go black, you never go back," quipped Ros, with a long, cheeky smile across her pretty face. (I never could understand her husband leaving her.) Stereotypes that laud other races and belittle white people, particularly white men, don't bother us. (Ros didn't speak from personal experience. The only men with whom she mentioned being involved were Australian.)

Sharon took offence that the chief financial officer Phil feared the prevalence of the human immunodeficiency virus among Africans, hoping he wore condoms. She took a little less offence, I think, at me saying she valued herself too little. There were times I felt guilty for having hired the taxi through which Sharon met the Nigerian, but if she'd not befriended him because of that trip then she'd have befriended someone else like him because of another taxi trip, or standing at a bus stop, or walking through a park.

"Multiracialism is okay," decided Sharon, as if race were separate from culture. "Multiculturalism is the problem." When Australia's immigration laws forced him back to Nigeria a few weeks after they'd met, she went there and married him. Immediately on her return to Australia, she took his surname. All she'd ever wanted was marriage. She married whomever she could.

Seven years after I last saw her, I noticed by chance Phil and his wife at the high school my eldest son and their two children attended. Last Phil had heard, Sharon was living with her Nigerian husband and their two children in Ashfield. I'd thus expect Sharon's story to be called something wonderful, introduced to her husband because of a five-minute taxi fare. If they were destitute or one had abandoned the other, we'd not mention it.

Years later, Sharon and I connected on social media. She and the Nigerian had divorced.

Not that anyone said so, but it was all rather sad. We should've treated Sharon better. She should've treated herself better.

20. RACIAL SUICIDE

We don't hear it said anymore, but black-and-white news footage from the 1960s or so reported an elegantly dressed woman giving her reason why Australia shouldn't allow interracial immigration. "It's not fair on the children," she said.

Interracial marriages were immoral for creating children without a people. Ending racial discrimination in immigration was much too important for us to worry about such unlikely events.

Besides, we soon stopped caring so much about children. We don't worry if they lack racial identities. So do we.

Other races worry. In 1979, Egypt became the first Arab country to sign a peace treaty with Israel. Following the 1990 Gulf War over Kuwait, many Egyptians living in Iraq went to Israel in search of work. Lawyer Nabil al-Wahsh estimated that over the ensuing two decades, thirty thousand Egyptian men married Israeli women, only about ten percent of whom were fellow Arabs. While Western lawyers oppose discrimination, Wahsh persuaded Supreme Administrative Court judge Mohammed al-Husseini in Cairo in 2010 to compel the Egyptian interior ministry to ask cabinet to take necessary steps to strip Egyptian men married to Israeli women, and their children, of Egyptian citizenship.

Tiny percentage as they were of almost eighty million Egyptians at the time, Wahsh had brought the case to prevent the creation in Egypt of mixed-race children "disloyal to Egypt and the Arab world," who "should not be allowed to perform their military service." Egypt's national interest was an Arab racial interest.

It's all very different for the West. We're individuals, not loyal to our race or countries, anyway.

Nevertheless, identity can be confusing for mixed-race children and the adults they become. "As a man, I've always felt Irish," said Harrison Ford in 2000. "As an actor, I've always felt Jewish." It was all very quaint, and agnostic Ford seemed relaxed about it, but one identity for part of his day and another for the rest is hardly identity. It's hardly belonging.

"I am a Eurasian," said Singaporean mixed-race Cheryl Frois in 2010, "so my roots are a bit more undefined." Eurasian is among the races on Singaporean identity cards, but mixed-race people lack racial identities. In a world where the only identities are racial (and, to a lesser extent, religious), they often lack identities altogether.

They also suffer biological complications. Britons and Hungarians mightn't appear particularly different racially, but Leukaemia patient Kate Raferty's Hungarian mother and white Australian father made her genetically unusual. In 2017, she struggled to find a donor for a bone marrow transplant to save her life.

Those transplants required a partial genetic match relating to an array of genes known as the H.L.A. system. "You inherit half of your H.L.A. type from your mother and half from your father," said Paul Berghoffer, operations manager with the Bone Marrow Donor Centre, "and because it is an entirely inherited trait, we find there are H.L.A. clusters within particular ethnic groups." Donors need to be of the same ethnicity as the patients. "Looking at the law of averages, it's definitely more challenging for people of mixed backgrounds to find a H.L.A. match."

Where families remain valued, mixed-race children are often outcasts, belonging not to two races but none. The West doesn't see that as reason for us to reconsider our attitudes to mixed-race relationships. For a friend of journalist Heidi Davoren in 2012, it was reason to adopt.

We used to talk of indigenous people being mixed-race or half-caste, before doing so became offensive (as the Western Australian Museum noted when I visited in 2010). That was too biological, scientific, and racist. Instead of being part indigenous, they're now indigenous or not. They can decide.

In the 1998 Australian Federal Court case of *Shaw v Wolf*, Jewish judge Ron Merkel thought democracy required a right to choose individual identity, as only the postmodern West does. "In a democratic society, individuals have the right to adopt such identity and culture as they may choose to adopt. Likewise, subject to human rights and equal opportunity legislation, communities in such a society are free to recognise or refuse to recognise the identities or cultures adopted by the various members of that society. Those are matters of sociology, and generally there should be little or no role for the law in that process."

Merkel quoted writers Sally Morgan and Roberta Sykes describing how they came to identify as indigenous. Aboriginal identity isn't just a matter of appearance, but also a complex combination of ancestry, self-identification, and community acceptance. "Aboriginality as such is not capable of any single or satisfactory definition," said Merkel. "Clearly the Aboriginality of persons who have retained their spiritual and cultural association with their land and past will differ fundamentally from the Aboriginality of those whose ancestors lost that association."

He made Aboriginality a matter of culture as much as biology, but to speak of ancestry is to recognise the biological framework of race. Mixed-race Aborigines choose their race from among the bloods they inherit, provided other Aborigines don't mind.

A decade later, journalist Andrew Bolt, whose parents immigrated from the Netherlands, wrote that mixed-race Aborigines looking all the world like Europeans identified as Aboriginal for political reasons, trying to be "*hip*," and helping their careers. There'd come to be great benefit in being black, much as there'd once been great disadvantage.

Aborigines were aghast. "*Under Bolt's rules*," wrote Chris Graham, editor of the *National Indigenous Times* newspaper, "*other people get to define your identity. Under Bolt's rules, all we are is how we look. Which is nonsense. There's more to human beings than their appearance. Race runs much deeper than skin colour.*"

Graham was right, but the reaction to Bolt's article wasn't simply correcting him. Worse than reporting matters that shouldn't be reported is expressing ideas that shouldn't be expressed. Merkel, who'd ceased being a judge in 2006, went onto be awarded a Human Rights Medal from the Human Rights Commission in 2011 for a lifetime's work including his advocacy in the successful Aboriginal lawsuit against Bolt and the *Herald Sun* newspaper publishing his comments. Bolt was found to have breached section 18C of the Racial Discrimination Act, prohibiting actions reasonably likely to offend another race.

We have freedom to choose our identity, but not freedom to talk about other people's choices. "*People have a right to decide for themselves whether or not they will identify as an Aboriginal Australian*," wrote Anthony Dillon, a university researcher and lecturer, in 2011, "*nobody else should determine it for them.*"

On the face of them, his words weren't limited to mixed-race

Aborigines. Dillon identified as an Aboriginal Australian.

Believing we're free to be whatever we want to be doesn't reach to all of us choosing our race. If we want to be Aborigines, then Aborigines have to accept our choice. Aboriginality for the mixed-race may be race defined by choice as much as biology, but it's biology nevertheless. Although steeped in personal choice, culture, and acceptance by other Aborigines, only those with some Aboriginal blood can apply.

The woman I married is British. Our children are British. There's nothing to choose. It makes identity simple.

Stepping back from our past sciences and more careful observation and analysis, skin and hair are the most visible measures of race. The daughter of a Fijian Indian and a New Zealander, Jacinta Lal won the Miss India New Zealand beauty contest in 2010, but being blonde with blue eyes, there were boos from the audience. Lal said later she "heard people saying, I wasn't Indian-looking enough to win the pageant."

We're accustomed to people of other races representing our countries, but these pageants were based upon race. Festival organiser Dharmesh Parikh acknowledged complaints questioning Lal's eligibility to be in the pageant.

"They shouldn't be doing that by looking at her hair or whatever," said Auckland Indian Association president Harshad Patel of the complainants. "She's Indian. She's got Indian blood... They should find out the facts. They should be more open-minded."

Race isn't a matter of physical appearance and other people's acceptance. It's a matter of blood: of biology and biological relationship.

Several countries host Miss India pageants, which only women carrying Indian blood can enter. Differentiated by their countries of residence, the winners compete in the Miss India Worldwide Pageant. The twenty-first pageant, in 2012, was held in Suriname.

Racial purity again came to the fore when mixed-race Torika Watters was crowned Miss World Fiji in 2012. Many Fijians believed she didn't look "native" enough. In particular, she lacked a *buiniga*, the naturally fuzzy Fijian hair. (Shortly after being awarded her crown, she lost it for being only sixteen years of age.)

When only one parent is Western, then the other normally defines their children, as it did when we enjoyed our racial identities. Being English was being purely English, and so forth. America's melting pot didn't make people American unless both parents were European, even North European. Anyone who wasn't purely white wasn't white at all, much like colours of paint mixed together.

My father spoke of people predominantly but not completely European having "a touch of the tar brush." Being European was like clean water that could only be soiled by adding anything else. Having lost our racial self-respect, being white became like white milk to which adding flavour meant we taste only the flavour.

"I've never thought of myself as biracial," said Princeton University professor Melissa Harris-Lacewell (later known as television hostess Melissa Harris-Perry) in 2007. Her father was black and mother white. "I'm black."

Barack Obama was the first African American president because his father was Kenyan, in spite of his white American mother. Venezuela's President Hugo Chavez also played down the Spanish parts of his ancestry. "We are not asking him to be a revolutionary, to be a socialist – no," Chavez told a political rally at the time of Obama's election in 2008; America and Venezuela had become adversaries in recent years. "I send an overture to the black man, from us here, who are of indigenous, black, Caribbean, South American race." Venezuela was a signatory to the 1965 International Convention on the Elimination of All Forms of Racial Discrimination.

Chavez's words quickly faded from earshot, as most words quickly fade in the West. They made me wonder why race couldn't bring white people together as it often brings other races together, overcoming national and political differences.

The darker race defines, not just with white people. Born to a black man and Thai woman, American golfer Tiger Woods was black. Only Thais noticed anything else.

Their mixed-race status remains. Appealing to white American voters, Obama called himself a "mutt" in 2008. Three years later, in July 2011, he repeated the sentiment on the American television programme *The View*. "We are a sort of mongrel people," he said of African Americans. "I mean we're all kinds of mixed up." In the multiracial West, being mixed up is more than just biology. "That's actually true of white people as well, but we just know more about it."

We who create the mongrels are just as cavalier. While helping at our sons' cub troop the first Monday of April 2012, Andrew, a Briton, mentioned that his first wife and mother of his first three children was Iranian. His second wife and mother of his fourth child was Filipina. "I'm doing my bit to mongrelise the gene pool," he said flippantly.

A recruiter from the Melbourne office of executive recruitment firm Egon Zehnder, with whom I spoke at a cocktail party in the Union, University and Schools Club, Sydney the second Tuesday in November 2010, spoke of the British race dying out altogether because of our lack of racial identity. Amidst a conversation about other races and their racial identities, he made his observation dispassionately. He, a Briton, wasn't so racist as to care.

Unfettered individualists don't care, but pillory those who do. Some welcome our demise, along with the rise of young populations.

Our customary blindness to race didn't prevent the *Sydney Morning Herald* newspaper picturing a Eurasian baby born in Sydney through the 1990s, I think, with an accompanying headline proclaiming something like 'We're creating a new race.' We trumpet our demise, our sweet self-destruction. We bask in the birth of a new race, without regard for the passing of ours.

Late in the first decade of the new millennium, a British news report enthused that the fastest-growing ethnic group in Britain are mixed-race whites and blacks, without mentioning the converse: the English are the most rapidly declining. Our new racism welcomes not just the end of our old racism but the end of our race; the end of our race is the end of our racism. More than willing to breed ourselves to extinction, we're eager to do so.

In 2011, South African photographer Mike Mike persuaded a hundred people in racially diverse Sydney to pose for his camera. He used computer modelling of the photographs to create his "Face of Tomorrow," by which white Australians disappear. "The process of merging the faces and coming up with someone new is really exciting," he said. The idea had come to him sitting on a London underground train and being intrigued by the racial diversity. "I thought if one could merge all the people in a place like London one would be looking at the future of that place – one would have some notion of what a Londoner is or will become." Britons disappear too.

With their racial identities, other races don't disappear. They in their countries remain.

Ironically, given all that's happened since then, our forebears feared that interracial relationships might breed out Aborigines; their genes being recessive (as my father once told me). Nevertheless, an Australian museum I visited, I think the Western Australian Museum, accused our forebears of plotting genocide because of it. If that was genocide, then so is the racial mixing that eradicates European races.

"This is the same kind of thought that underpinned horrific crimes like the Nazis," cried out Sam Watson, the deputy director of the Aboriginal and Torres Strait Islander Studies Unit at the University of Queensland in 2009. He was referring specifically to a biscuit, Creole Creams, containing brown chocolate and white vanilla. "The word 'Creole' comes from a period when people's humanity was measured by the amount of white blood they had in their bloodstream."

The biscuits had stood on supermarket shelves for three years before Watson discovered them. Perhaps, like Nova Peris, he preferred Tim Tams.

"People need to exercise their intellect," said Watson, without any obvious sense of irony. "This so-called blending was actually the institutionalised rape of black women. They were victims of brutal regimes of rape and victimisation."

Thomas Jefferson may well have condemned slavery privately, but he didn't just own slaves. He slept with one, Sally Hemmings, many years after his wife's death. She was his late wife's half-sister.

Watson could have been describing interracial relationships involving someone from a dominant culture, as we say we are. Interracial relations between people of a dominant culture and those of other cultures are institutional rape. Like managers with employees and doctors with patients, their inequality of power means there can be no real consent.

The Creole Cream biscuit represented a "deep undercurrent of racism in white Australian society," explained Watson, although I doubt most white Australians would have known what a creole was. I needed to look into the term. "It virtually infects every level of Australia's consciousness, language, culture, and history."

Other races have their race. We have racism.

Coles supermarkets insisted creole referred only to a cuisine, but backed down at great cost. Goodness knows what Watson made of meringues.

We to whom individualism is paramount are killing the politic within us. Without societies there can be no social suicide, but we are the body suicide. Genocide never contemplated races committing racial suicide, but we don't consider what we're doing genocide because we've decided we're not a race or races anyway. There's nothing to eradicate. The truth of being a people dies before a people does, leading by whatever turns and motivations to our stupid suicide.

21. SELF-RESPECT

There was a time, centuries ago, that European fashion was to powder our skins whiter: the whitest shades of pale. Those powders were dangerous and we learnt not to use them, but we liked to be white. Particularly in the colonies with the warmest of climes, women carried umbrellas to save their skin from the sun, although a touch of sun became evidence of wealth enough for exotic holidays abroad. Men wore hats.

The Holocaust drove from us much of our sense of beauty in naturally white skin, not to mention blond hair and blue eyes. We came to call ourselves colour-blind and might even achieve it, but not about us. We darkened our skins in the sun, exhorting sun-tanned bodies as our most beautiful of forms, without worrying until recently about cancer risks.

Our attitudes to ourselves became other people's attitudes to us. "You're so white," several boys at our local high school told my eldest son, intending to insult him.

"I saw you on the news as pale as ever," Arian said to him when he was thirteen years old, after a television station broadcast our family preparing for the first day of the 2009 school year.

While none are dedicated to European peoples, quite a few beauty contests around the world are defined by the contestants' race. Miss Philippines U.S.A. reached the news in 2013 because a contestant, Joanlia Lising, answered a question so nonsensically. Contestants for Miss Philippines Australia don't qualify because they've been to Manila.

Those races dwell upon the beauty they see in their own. In 2012, thirty-two countries competed in the International Miss Lebanon pageant in Beirut, including the twelfth Miss Lebanon Australia, Deedee Zibara. "The Arab eye is beautiful," said Monie Gabriel, the Australian event's head of beauty, "and we like to accentuate the eye with dark eyeliner and eye extensions."

Lebanese are no less at each other's throats in beauty pageants than anywhere else. "The pageant is not about politics but about beauty, heritage, contribution to community," said director of Miss Lebanon Australia, Joe Khoury. "It's only a few in the Lebanese community causing trouble. Every community has the same problem."

Following past scandal and to reduce allegations of corruption or bribery, businesswoman Norah Blackman instigated a rule that "no one on the judging panel is to be Arabic or have a Lebanese background, whatsoever." She was Arab.

A black woman on a crowded London bus was the subject of a film recording two and a half minutes long that surfaced in August 2012. "I'm so glad I'm born black and I'll die black," she shouted at other passengers. "My parents are f***ing African, born in Jamaica, and I'm f***ing African, born in England and I can't stand you white people, I tell you."

Britain's efforts to eradicate race didn't impress her. "I don't care what none of you lot got to say," she told the white people around her, "because at the end of the day, if you lot would have had a choice you will f***ing go with your people and I'll go with mine." (We don't have a choice.) "The whole lot of you are programmed, f***ing puppets. Not this one, I'm black and proud." She wasn't changing her racial appearance as white people were. "They all want to be f***ing black. They all put fat in their lips and their bottoms and sit down on the sunbed to be black." (Tanning salons mean little except to white people and paler-skinned Eurasians.) "Strictly black: the more black, the happier I am."

Police spoke with the woman. I could find no reports of the outcome. I couldn't even learn her name.

By 2013, America's changing race meant Arizona gubernatorial candidate Fred DuVal darkened his skin in his campaign advertisements to appear Hispanic. He would claim it was a joke.

We've come back to where we started. The coloureds who became Negroes when science came to fore and then became Africans when we focussed upon geographical origins are again people of colour. It makes them sound more fun than us colourless whites.

While white people escape our skin colour (or lack of colour, if we will), people from other races try to imitate the race we're trying not to be. In 2002, dermatologists Pascal Del Giudice and Pinier Yves reported their study of six hundred and eighty-five Senegalese women in Dhaka in 1992 and '93. Pursuing the fairest colours they could, thirty-six percent had used skin-whitening products. Twenty-six percent still used them.

White women tan their skins. Indian women avoid the sun to avoid becoming browner.

"Lots of Indians, Sri Lankans, and Pakistanis play in the early stages of cricket," said Lisa Sthalekar in 2009, explaining why she was a rare Indian playing in the Australian women's cricket team, "but many of them drop out when it gets serious to focus more on their work." (Hers was a racial generalisation, but nobody minds other races complimenting themselves.) "It's also the case, certainly in women's cricket, that a lot of Indians don't want to get any darker, and so they don't want to spend any more time in the sun than they have to."

In India, Indian women lather their skins with creams to make them lighter. Pregnant rural women consume dairy products believing their babies will be lighter skinned. Darker-skinned models and actresses struggle for work.

"If some Jews used to suffer self-hatred," wrote Indian journalist Amrit Dhillon in 2012, *"at least you knew it was because previous generations had undergone persecution for centuries. If some African Americans used to have low esteem and tried to lighten their skin and straighten their hair, at least you knew that a history of slavery must have cast a shadow on their confidence. But what can explain this Indian hatred of the colour of their own skin? Yes, I know that the British Raj was white, but Mughal rule in India lasted much longer and the Mughals were not white, so the 'colonial complex' theory doesn't quite do the job. If the theory were correct, Indians would hanker after slanted eyes as the Mughals were Mongols from Central Asia, but Indians refer to their own people from the north-east disparagingly as 'chinky-eyed'."*

Her writing was the first I'd read of India being ruled by anyone but the British and the first I'd heard of Indians being racially prejudiced against other Asians. Dhillon's concern wasn't her people's derision towards other races, but their derision towards their own. *"Just as African Americans launched a Black is Beautiful campaign in the US, so India needs a similar self-affirming movement. Fast."*

In the 1930s and '40s, black American psychologists Kenneth and Mamie Clark found black American girls preferred white dolls to black ones. They associated white dolls with niceness and prettiness, but black ones with being bad and ugly. The difference was less pronounced in racially integrated schools than in racially segregated schools, which was cited in court cases ordering racial integration from the 1950s. The short 2005 documentary *A Girl Like Me* repeated the survey, reporting similar results after half a century of racial integration.

The meaning of the results is unclear. They might simply suggest the girls found white people to be nicer than black people. (We, of course, reject any such notion. If the girls thought as much, we'd decry whatever white racism we're certain created such impressions.) They might have lacked racial self-respect.

"There are a lot of young black girls who I meet in my travels who don't have a lot of self-esteem," said black American singer Lauryn Hill in 1999. "So if I communicate to them that they're beautiful, no white person should find fault in that. It doesn't mean that young white girls aren't beautiful, because they are just as beautiful." In the words of the May 1999 edition of *Teen People* magazine, "*Lauryn insists she wants people to understand that her goal to improve the self-love of young African-American women should never be confused with advocating racial supremacy.*"

I would say the same to white men and women, girls and boys. Loving ourselves for being Irish or British, Polish or Czech, or more broadly European, doesn't have to be synonymous with a sense of racial supremacy. White people valuing their race aren't impugning anyone.

We've become the people who think no one else is good enough for us and people who think no one else will have us. We think we're beautiful because we hide below colours in our hair and thicker colours on our face or we wear too many or few clothes, never realising how beautiful we are in spite of them. (The most beautiful men and women are those most worried about their beauty.) We love so many wondrous things, but fail to love ourselves.

We've become prejudiced against us and our kind, pounding ourselves with self-hating racism. Our opposition to white people's racism requires us to denigrate ourselves.

We make negative generalisations about nationalities, provided they're predominantly white. We'll talk of Western countries being anything bad, without dwelling upon other races being the same. American travel company Expedia surveyed hoteliers to determine the most popular and unpopular tourists from a group of twenty-seven nationalities. Reports of the results published in 2009 focused upon the unpopularity of French tourists more than the unpopularity of Chinese.

The Sunday night my wife, baby son, and I spent in Ullapool in September 1996, we watched a television programme mentioning a survey asking Britons their greatest complaint about Americans. The answer, a contestant guessed correctly, was that Americans were loud.

Such a survey asking Britons their complaints about Indians, Pakistanis, or West Indians would've been incomprehensible. About Americans, it was television.

They meant white Americans, although the American-accented Malays bundling around a Malaysian city during my time there were just as loud and more arrogant. Whether they were American born or learnt their language from Americans, I don't know.

When other races feel ashamed of their race, we counsel them, pleading with them to be proud of their skin tones and cherish their colours. If I were to cry how beautiful black, Asian, or Islander people are, they'd smile fondly. So would we.

When Hong Kong and other Chinese parents sent their children to the prestigious private girls' school at which my wife was a teacher, they expected their children to be in the best classes because they assumed Australians were fools. One Chinese mother told the school it was fortunate her daughter was there. No number of mediocre academic results by their daughters changed their views.

East Asians don't need to exhort pride in their race. We refuse to feel pride in ours.

American Chinese woman Amy Chua and her Jewish husband Jed Rubenfeld went so far as to say eight races and cultural groups (including Chinese and Jews) are inherently better than others in their 2014 book *Triple Package Culture*. Among the reasons for their success, they argued, is their sense of racial superiority. Little wonder then that Europeans (other than Mormons) aren't among the successful races, not anymore.

We used to be. As was the norm until World War II, America's President Abraham Lincoln was a racist. Condemning slavery isn't condemning racism.

"I will say, then," he said, in his fourth debate with the Democratic Party's Stephen Douglas on the eighteenth day of September 1858, "that I am not, nor have ever been, in favour of bringing about in any way the social and political equality of the black and white races – that I am not, nor ever have been, in favour of making voters or jurors of Negroes, nor of qualifying them to hold office, nor to intermarry with white people, and I will say in addition to this that there is a physical difference between the white and black races, which will ever forbid the two races living together on terms of social and political equality, and inasmuch as they cannot so live, while they do remain together, there must be the position of superior and inferior, and I, as much as any other man, am in favour of having the superior position assigned to the white race."

We once believed North Europeans to be biologically superior to other races. We've become hostile to such a suggestion.

A book blaming anyone but white men for the problems of the world would be sexist and racist, as would a book crediting white men with anything good. Michael Moore, a white American, titled his 2001 book about President George W. Bush and his administration *Stupid White Men*. Rather than imagine other people being a problem, he designated Bush's influential national security adviser Condoleezza Rice, a black woman, an honorary stupid white male; some honour.

Moore's book sold half a million copies. He wasn't stupid.

Anthony Sharwood's review of the 2012 television series *The Shire* made Moore's diatribe seem like adoration. After enthusing for the "*modern day ethnic patchwork quilt that is Australia*," he mocked the "*white, vacuous, botoxed minority*" uncommonly prevalent in the Sutherland Shire. Sharwood was white, although presumably didn't see himself as being vacuous or the beneficiary of Botox injections. (He didn't mention the Shire having the lowest crime rate of any local government area in Sydney.)

We abandon our fixation with equality to consider ourselves intrinsically inferior. It's simpler. By doing so, we recognise racial comparisons, but without any scientific rigour or the discipline of logic. Facts don't lead us to malign other races or keep us from maligning our own. Uniquely among the races of earth, we feel that not espousing our cultural, aesthetic, or other inferiority equates to some boot-stomping sense of being superior.

We might now be morally inferior. Wantonly we betray our forebears, families, and each other. There's something evil about hating those among our race caring for us.

Racial bigotry is never more ironic than when cloaked in the show of lambasting racism. Racial hatred is no less hatred because we hate our own. We dumb whiteys are more stupid than ever, destroying our value in ourselves. We think we're distinct from the rest of our race when it's race by which we malign each other, but by race, we malign ourselves. Western self-bigotry we might call our fight against racism, but it's a fight against our race. Our inversion of racism is still racism. Ours are the politics of self-abuse.

It's more than our comeuppance for a past in which we felt superior to other races. We've driven from us, and had driven from us, any sense of self-esteem as no other race in history has suffered, much as the Jews must've felt by 1945. Completely comfortable with shaming ourselves down, we're frightened to stop. If Nazi Germany's claims of racial superiority justified the Jewish Holocaust, then our new-found reeking of racial inferiority justifies our racial suicide.

Wanting to survive doesn't require a sense of superiority. It does require some sense of self-worth. There's no shying away from the fact that wanting our race to survive is racist, not just for recognising race but for being loyal to our own. I've never met a racist I didn't like.

Restoring our self-respect isn't conservatism. It's restoration. We need only believe we're as worthy as other races of self-respect.

If all of us think of our families, then that would be enough. We could be kind, allowing for ourselves the racial compliments we confer upon others: seeing the rich beauty in blue-water eyes, holding out our arms and enjoying our silken white skin. Even I cringe a little embarrassed to say no woman is more beautiful than my wife like a white English rose. From our families, our peoples flow.

The most daunting of problems are solvable, if not by individuals. Some require families, peoples, and nations. The reality remains that a world without white people will be less able and willing to feed, house, and clothe people: to deal with challenges and threats of any kind. It will accomplish fewer fine arts and less in the sciences, produce fewer ideas and philosophies. The world would be less beautiful.

22. HITLER'S WRATH

With his black hair and pointed features, Nazi dictator Adolf Hitler was no blond, square-jawed personification of the Aryan racial greatness he vaunted. He embodied Germans much less than most leaders embody the people they lead. He never bore children, although I can't recall where I heard that was because he knew he was no human ideal. The idea made him seem noble, a self-sacrificing hero, except that self-hatred is neither noble nor heroic.

Hitler's racism was more complex than people assume racism to be. Genocide requires much, much more than mere racism.

Certain that Hitler's oratory and Joseph Goebbels' propaganda played roles in the Holocaust, a line often attributed to them has been: If you're going to lie, make it a big one. It implies their talk of Aryan superiority and Jewish and other inferiority was a lie and a big lie at that. It casts Hitler and Goebbels as proud liars, gloating over a hapless populace believing them. It's another reason to reject racism, if not even Hitler and Goebbels believed it.

Eventually, I began thinking about those words and the men reportedly saying them. I did something I dare say few of us do: I looked into the circumstances in which they said them.

Hitler wrote them in chapter 10 of *Mein Kampf*, a book difficult to obtain early in the twenty-first century. "*All this was inspired by the principle – which is quite true in itself – that in the big lie there is always a certain force of credibility; because the broad masses of a nation are always more easily corrupted in the deeper strata of their emotional nature than consciously or voluntarily; and thus in the primitive simplicity of their minds they more readily fall victims to the big lie than the small lie, since they themselves often tell small lies in little matters but would be ashamed to resort to large-scale falsehoods. It would never come into their heads to fabricate colossal untruths, and they would not believe that others could have the impudence to distort the truth so infamously. Even though the facts which prove this to be so may be brought clearly to their minds, they will still doubt and waver and will continue to think that there may be some other explanation. For the grossly impudent lie always leaves traces behind it, even after it has been nailed down, a fact which is known to all expert liars in this world and to all who conspire together in the art of lying. These people know only too well how to use falsehood for the basest purposes."*

His words damned him, until I read the next paragraph. *"From time immemorial, however, the Jews have known better than any others how falsehood and calumny can be exploited. Is not their very existence founded on one great lie, namely, that they are a religious community, whereas in reality they are a race? And what a race! One of the greatest thinkers that mankind has produced has branded the Jews for all time with a statement which is profoundly and exactly true. He (Schopenhauer) called the Jew "The Great Master of Lies." Those who do not realise the truth of that statement, or do not wish to believe it, will never be able to lend a hand in helping Truth to prevail."*

There was, of course, no end of other acts to damn Hitler, but it's untrue of his critics to say he proudly peddled lies. He wrote in *Mein Kampf* of pursuing the truth, following a long line of European and particularly German philosophy seeking facts and truths, but we're no longer espousing anything Europeans and particularly Germans did. In our rush to reject Hitler's philosophies we rejected notions of truth, although far more people than Hitler through Western history sought truth.

For good measure, I went onto check whether the philosopher Arthur Schopenhauer called the Jew: *"The Great Master of Lies."* He did. That doesn't mean it was true, but that Schopenhauer believed it was true. Schopenhauer was an atheist and early proponent of animal rights, who died almost three decades before Hitler was born.

Goebbels wrote of the big lie in an article titled 'From Churchill's Lie Factory' in *Die Zeit ohne Beispiel* on the second Sunday in January 1941, when England and Germany were at war. *"One should not as a rule reveal one's secrets,"* he wrote, *"since one does not know if and when one may need them again. The essential English leadership secret does not depend on particular intelligence. Rather, it depends on a remarkably stupid thick-headedness. The English follow the principle that when one lies, one should lie big, and stick to it. They keep up their lies, even at the risk of looking ridiculous."*

For Goebbels, the big lie was the Englishman's lie: Winston Churchill's lie. It related to war with Germany.

Whether people are lying or sincere but mistaken in what they say is difficult to know, unless they admit to lying. We can't enter their heads to see. To say Hitler and Goebbels proudly peddled big lies is itself a big lie. If it's not a big lie, then it's a big mistake.

Often accompanying the claim that Nazis lied is that Nazi anti-Semitism made Jews scapegoats for Germany's problems. Sometime in the early 1990s I think it was, I watched a television documentary programme with rare colour film of pre-war Germany. Instead of the usual grainy black-and-white images of the time that distort reality into antiquity, the colour was more real than my postmodern world. The festival faces enjoying a German cultural carnival in Munich, the summer of 1939, portrayed Germany happier than I'd seen Europe since then.

The images were extraordinarily eerie. These were our wartime enemy, my lifetime enemy, but good men, women, and children that last summer. Nazi soldiers were as friendly as the amicable police officers of London, keeping the peace, without thoughts of genocide.

My most poignant memory from the documentary was of Hitler privately saying something to the effect that he hadn't achieved all he'd achieved just for festivals. The words made him seem like many other political leaders, but for what happened through the ensuing months and years.

Germany had been a mess when Hitler came to power in 1933. By 1939, Germany was prospering. Without problems there's no need for scapegoats. The most that could be said was that Hitler accredited Germany's ability to rebuild herself anew upon disenfranchising the Jews (and others) or that he feared future Jewish influence. If he was making the Jews scapegoats, then it was for problems passed or that might arise in the future. It's a strange use of the term.

People don't kill scapegoats. They keep them alive to continue being scapegoats.

Seeing such prosperity, and my schoolboy studies of history and other learning, makes it hard to accept any quick and tidy explanation for Nazi anti-Semitism. Hitler appears to have enjoyed many Jewish friends while living in Vienna before the Great War, in spite of other Viennese then fearing being overrun by East European Jews. Most historians believe his anti-Semitism arose after World War I because he blamed Jews (along with Germany's political leadership and communists) for Germany's calamitous defeat.

Incredibly I thought when first I read of it, preparing for my time in Czechoslovakia in 1986, Hitler ordered the collection of Jewish items in Prague to form a museum of Jewish culture. Studying the synagogues, golden candleholders, and pebbles rested atop gravestones in a crowded cemetery, my Roman Catholic girlfriend and Protestant I learnt more about Judaism there than any Jew I'd met had taught me, and probably more than most Jews I'd met knew. If there'd never been races then there'd have never been a Jewish Holocaust, but nor would there have been Jewish culture. In Hitler's European vision, Jews didn't need to survive for us to learn about them.

All in all, it's unlikely Nazi anti-Semitism was a political scheme. More likely was that Nazis genuinely believed anti-Semitism to be Germany defending her interests.

"We had the moral right," Heinrich Himmler told those hundred *Schutzstaffel* group leaders in Posen, the first Monday of October 1943, "we had the duty to our people, to destroy this people which wanted to destroy us." Yet with Germany's defeat imminent in April 1945, Himmler met with a representative of the World Jewish Congress to free four and a half thousand prisoners, half of them Jewish, from the women's concentration camp at Ravensbrück. With Germany doomed anyway, Himmler saw no reason to kill those prisoners.

Germans enjoyed senses of survival, loyalty, and morality, likely thinking as much in terms of Europe and even humanity; European peoples tend to think on behalf of humanity. Not content to leave the rest of Europe to suffer, the Nazi leadership believed they'd all fare better without Jews, gypsies, and the like. What Hitler called the Jewish problem required a final solution. Unlike other anti-Semitism, he attempted genocide.

It was extreme nationalism but nationalism, extreme racism but racism: quite real, not a lie. Since then, we've not tried so hard to kill a lie. We're not opposing racism merely as a political tool.

Like Himmler, Hitler considered himself good: an idealist trying to make the world better. He was a hero in his head, much as we are in our heads when we oppose racism.

Hitler's family hinted at genetic disorder; in his Austrian childhood home was a schizophrenic hunchback, his Aunt Johanna. As if there could be no end to the fierce irony that such a man should espouse racial purification was the chance Hitler was racially part Jewish.

Psychologist Alice Miller was a Jewess born in Poland, who never met Hitler let alone interviewed him, but she drew upon evidence from people who had in her 1980 book *For Your Own Good*. As a boy, Hitler suffered at the hands of his tyrannical father Alois, who Miller theorised abused his son because he was tortured by the pain of being an illegitimate child from an affair between his German mother Maria Schickelgruber and a nineteen-year-old Jew named Frankenberger. Alois' pain, Miller theorised, became Adolf's.

Nazi Germany's race laws were more severe than those in other countries. Had Hitler been subject to the same laws as other Germans, then he may well have died in the Holocaust.

When Austria became part of the greater German Reich, following the Anschluss in 1938, German tanks destroyed the birthplaces of Alois Hitler and Alois' mother. Hitler might've been eradicating evidence of his Jewish ancestry or of mental illness in his family, or he might have just hated his father and grandmother.

Miller theorised that the possibility he was a quarter Jewish tormented Adolf Hitler, although Frankenberger might not have even existed. All that's clear is that the Nuremberg race laws of 1935 defined Jews to be those with at least one Jewish grandparent. With his father's name left blank on Alois Hitler's birth certificate, Adolf Hitler couldn't prove he wasn't a second-degree Jew. To deal with the problem, the Nuremberg laws explicitly exempted Adolf Hitler. (They also, for that matter, exempted Jesus Christ.)

Adding to the complexity of Nazi anti-Semitism, the Nuremberg race laws also exempted Jews militarily decorated during the Great War, including *Leutnant* Hugo Gutmann, the holder of an Iron Cross, First Class, whose story my friend Barry told me. Gutmann recommended Hitler also be awarded an Iron Cross, First Class, during the war, needing to argue strongly that a mere corporal should receive an honour usually accorded only officers. Hitler had already won the Iron Cross, Second Class, but Gutmann's recommendation helped.

The exemption from the Nuremberg race laws granted those decorated soldiers didn't apply to their families. For his family's sake, Gutmann fled, but Hitler approved Germany continuing to pay him his pension after he reached America in 1939.

Hitler didn't hate all Jews. Racism is a collective racial identity, distinct from the treatment of individuals within a race (as our new-found individualism can't comprehend). As well as the categories of exemptions from the Nuremberg race laws, individual Jews exempted included Erich Milch, whom Hitler declared an honorary Aryan. Milch was one of two Jews among the thirty or so field marshals in Hitler's armies. In those armies were thousands more Jews.

None of these facts alleviate Hitler's guilt. They do make anti-Semitism more complicated than simplistic villainy or a maniacal hatred of Jews.

In spite of so much and so many stacked against her, Germany came close to winning World War II. By early 1945, she was facing defeat. Brave Germans had suffered horrors in Stalingrad and elsewhere among the impoverished, wounded, and dead men and women, but Hitler turned on the German people he blamed for failing him. On the third Monday of March 1945, he ordered the destruction of what remained of German industry, communications, and transport systems. If he were to die, Germany should be destroyed. Whatever he thought about Jews, Hitler came to want the destruction of Germany.

Across the West, among vanquished and victors alike, rulers came to hold their races in the same contempt. Soon enough, so did the ruled.

Predictions about Europeans fading away don't normally attract attention, but they did in 2002. German scientists reportedly predicted that naturally blond people would die out within two hundred years, with the last of them born in Finland. Subsequent news reports pointed out that no such research had been carried out, although blond people were forecast to become fewer along with the general decline of European populations. They called the story a hoax, with genes for blondness stronger than it claimed, but in the words of Lawrence Altman's report for the *New York Times* newspaper, it had been "*too good to check.*"

Not so widely reported are the uniquely European, particularly Scottish, red-headed people becoming fewer. Already making up less than two percent of the world's people, within a hundred years they could be extinct.

Several generations after his death too slow coming, Hitler would seem to be enjoying victory, after all. He inspired a Germany and Europe haunted by the ghosts of Holocaust to follow him into oblivion, succeeding destruction with our self-destruction. As I write, we're only wounded, but many of our wounds are self-inflicted. There may again be eras so dire for us, but I trust never again one when we work so hard by our acts and attitude against us. Our rejection of racism matters more than our race, to the end.

We confuse race with murder. So determined are we to avoid committing another Holocaust killing other races, we accept a Western Holocaust. If our prejudices lie dormant through all our tolerance to be reawakened by people and circumstances inspiring us, as they awoke in tolerant Germany in the 1920s and '30s with such effect, then the world will only be rid of Western prejudice when it's rid of Western peoples, we men and women capable of being Nazis. Other races will still be racist, but they've not killed Jews as we killed Jews, not recently anyway, not yet.

We're prisoners of war imprisoned in the camps of Auschwitz, until we die convinced we're finally free. Hitler never achieved his genocide of Jews, but more cruelly than he could have dreamed, the genocide of Germans and other European peoples is under way. To whatever extent our suicide isn't of our doing but the result of other people's hands and propaganda, theirs is the worst act of genocide in history. Manipulating us to die is murder.

BIBLIOGRAPHY, REFERENCES

Articles

Adams, Stephen, 'Addicted to the internet? It could be all in your genes,' *The Telegraph* newspaper, 31 August 2012.

Adams, Stephen, 'Breastfed babies 'more intelligent,' *The Telegraph* newspaper, 13 March 2012.

Alexander, Harriet, 'My children are all related – by love and commitment,' *The Telegraph* newspaper, 16 November 2013.

Anderson, Jennifer, 'Schools beat the drum for equity,' *Portland Tribune* newspaper, 6 September 2012. Paul Sperry, 'Obama collecting personal data for a secret race database,' *New York Post* newspaper, 18 July 2015.

Bita, Natasha, 'Ban on naughty corner, easter egg hunts,' *The Australian* newspaper, 4 April 2011. Dan Harrison, 'Minister sends fines idea to naughty corner,' *The Sydney Morning Herald* newspaper, 5 April 2011.

Blade, 'Danish sperm donor passes genetic disorder to five children,' *Agence France-Presse* news service published at *France 24*, 24 September 2012.

Booth, Lauren, 'Lauren Booth reveals why she HATES her mother and never wants to see her again,' *Daily Mail* newspaper, 21 March 2008. Uncredited, 'Blair sister-in-law urges war crimes trial,' *Agence France-Presse* news service published at *News Limited Network*, 26 January 2011.

Boshoff, Alison, 'Natasha's ski-fall tragedy: Struck down by the eternal curse of the Redgraves,' *Daily Mail* newspaper, 18 March 2009.

Bratskeir, Kate, 'People Who Order Coffee Black Are More Likely To Be Psychopaths,' *The Huffington Post* website, 12 October 2015.

Brown, Larisa, 'Woman arrested after video surfaces of black woman making racist comments about white people on a London bus,' *Daily Mail* newspaper, 20 August 2012.

Browne, Anthony, 'UK whites will be minority by 2100,' *The Observer* newspaper, 3 September 2000. Christopher Hope, 'U.K. cities to have white minorities in 30 years,' *The Telegraph* newspaper, 17 September 2007.

Budd, Henry with *Australian Associated Press* news service, 'Ceasar

Galea named as seventh nursing home fire death,' *The Daily Telegraph* newspaper, 21 November 2011. Jamelle Wells, 'Nursing home fire killer Dean 'won ethics prize',' *Australian Broadcasting Corporation News*, 17 June 2013.

Burns, Monica and Jessica Sommerville, "'I pick you': the impact of fairness and race on infants' selection of social partners,' *Frontiers in Psychology* journal, 12 February 2014. Molly McElroy, 'Babies prefer fairness – but only if it benefits them – in choosing a playmate,' *University of Washington news release*, 14 April 2014.

Casamento, Jo, 'New 'baby' helps to heal soap star Ada's marriage, *The Sydney Morning Herald* newspaper, 10 October 2010.

Choi, Charles, 'I Feel Your Pain, unless you're from a Different Race,' *Live Science*, 27 May 2010.

Corderoy Amy, 'East beats West when it comes to road manners and safety,' *The Sydney Morning Herald* newspaper, 17 June 2010.

Correspondents in New York, 'Ladies, your email address is a clue to your weight,' *The Sunday Telegraph* newspaper, 11 March 2011.

Coulter, Ann, 'Speed Kills Racial Profiling Study,' *The Daily Caller*, 3 September 2014. Uncredited, 'N.J. releases controversial racial speeding study,' *Cable News Network*, 2 April 2002.

Daffey, Paul, 'Lin's landing,' *Australian Football League Network*, 13 August 2012.

Davies, Justine, 'Are you 'wealthist'?' *Money Stuff* at *News Limited Network*, 27 February 2012.

Davoren, Heidi (writing as Dirty Laundry), 'The black and white of it,' *The Sydney Morning Herald* newspaper, 15 May 2012.

Del Giudice, Pascal and Pinier Yves, 'The widespread use of skin lightening creams in Senegal: a persistent public health problem in West Africa,' *International Journal of Dermatology*, Volume 41, Issue 2, February 2002.

Devine, Miranda, 'Swap pet sounds for a companionable silence,' *The Sydney Morning Herald* newspaper, 13 April 2008, concerning the money people spend on their pets and the impact of pets on greenhouse gas emissions. Miranda Devine, 'Unleashed, dog owners bite back,' *The Sydney Morning Herald* newspaper, 17 April 2008, concerning local councils setting aside parks for dogs and mentioning a region of Spain voting to give legal human rights to apes.

Dhillon, Amrit, 'The Indian obsession with fairer skin sinks to a new low,' *The Sydney Morning Herald* newspaper, 23 May 2012.

Elliott, Tim and others, 'Australian cricket 'needs ethnic stars',' *The Sydney Morning Herald* newspaper, 25 August 2009.

Elston, Laura, 'Kate's background is a mixed heritage,' *The Sydney Morning Herald* newspaper, 17 November 2010.

Even, Dan, 'Angelina Jolie's 'Jewish genetic mutation': Breast cancer gene is common in Israel, but few opt for preventive mastectomy,' *Haaretz* daily newspaper, 16 May 2013.

Gardiner, Stephanie, 'Drowned man hailed a hero after saving 10-year-old,' *The Sydney Morning Herald* newspaper, 7 November 2011.

Gilhooly, Joanne, 'Italy: Immigration or extinction,' *British Broadcasting Corporation News*, 19 April 2000.

Giubilini, Alberto and Francesca Minerva, 'After-birth abortion: why should the baby live?' *Journal of Medical Ethics*, 23 February 2012. Stephen Adams, 'Killing babies no different from abortion, experts say,' *The Telegraph* newspaper, 29 February 2012.

Goebbels, Joseph, *Aus Churchills Lügenfabrik (From Churchill's Lie Factory)*, *Die Zeit ohne Beispiel*. Munich: *Zentralverlag der Nationalsozialistische Deutsche Arbeiterpartei*, 12 January 1941.

Goins, Christopher, 'V.A. A.G. Fears D.C. Law May Relocate Rat 'Families' to Virginia,' *Cybercast News Service*, 13 January 2012.

Gridneff, Ilya, 'Night of big hair and lashes as contestants vie for Miss Lebanon crown,' *The Sydney Morning Herald* newspaper, 30 April 2012.

Gutowski, Stephen, 'Video Game Allows Players to Slaughter 'Tea Party Zombies' Like Sarah Palin and Bill O'Reilly,' *Media Research Centre Television*, 6 September 2011.

Ham, Becky, 'For Better and Worse, Chimpanzee Minds Are Much Like Ours,' *American Association for the Advancement of Science News Archive*, 14 February 2013. Uncredited, 'European Court agrees to hear chimp's plea for human rights,' *Evening Standard* newspaper, 21 May 2008.

Hassan, Iman, 'The dynamics of an African family,' *Africa on the Blog* website, 23 May 2013.

Haussegger, Virginia, 'Blundering Nelson spoils the mood of a healing day,' *The Canberra Times* newspaper, 16 February 2008, republished on her website.

Henderson, Michelle, 'Genetics 'could improve' Aboriginal health,'

Australian Associated Press news service published at *News Limited Network*, 2 July 2012.

Hinds, Richard, 'Football royalty put bucks before loyalty to crack the codes,' *The Sydney Morning Herald* newspaper, 4 December 2012.

Hodson, Gordon and Michael Busseri, 'Ideology and Low Intergroup Contact – Bright Minds and Dark Attitudes: Lower Cognitive Ability Predicts Greater Prejudice Through Right-Wing,' *Psychological Science* journal, Volume 23, 5 January 2012. Stephanie Pappas, 'Low I.Q. & Conservative Beliefs Linked to Prejudice,' *Live Science*, 26 January 2012.

Hoe Yeen Nie, 'Singaporeans of mixed race allowed to 'double barrel' race in I.C.,' *Channel News Asia*, 12 January 2010. Ben Winsor, 'Why mixed-race minorities struggle to find life-saving transplant matches,' *Special Broadcasting Service News*, 31 March 2017.

Hoey, Joshua, 'Coles backs down over 'racist' biscuit,' *The Brisbane Times* newspaper, 27 October 2009.

Horin, Adele, 'She once escaped a killer – under today's laws she would still be trapped,' *The Sydney Morning Herald* newspaper, 7 April 2011.

Howie, Emily, 'Admitting our racism problem is first step to a solution,' *The Sydney Morning Herald* newspaper, 7 September 2010.

Kanai, Ryota and others, 'Political Orientations Are Correlated with Brain Structure in Young Adults,' *Current Biology* journal, Volume 21, Issue 8, 26 April 2011. Correspondents in Washington, 'Brains differ in liberals, conservatives,' *Agence France-Presse* news service published at *News Limited Network*, 8 April 2011.

Kluger, Jeffrey, 'James Watson, Co-Discoverer of D.N.A.'s Double Helix, Leaves Behind a Troubling Legacy', *Time* magazine, 7 November 2025. See also Nigel Jones, 'James Watson deserved better', *Spectator* magazine, 8 November 2025.

Kwek, Glenda, 'Enter the dragons: why birth rate will soar,' *The Sydney Morning Herald* newspaper.

Labbé, Theola, 'Professor Melissa Harris-Lacewell sparks the conversation, in class and out,' *Princeton University*, 9 May 2007.

Lee, Julian, 'Steve Jobs's Apple legacy may not be so sweet at the core,' *The Sydney Morning Herald* newspaper, 31 August 2011.

Lewis, Jamie, 'Here come the brides: Spanish town takes drastic action to end 'bride shortage',' *The Independent* newspaper, 22 April 2012.

Loveys, Kate, ''Racists' aged THREE: Toddlers among thousands of children accused of bigotry after name-calling,' *Daily Mail* newspaper, 14 September 2011.

Lucas, Fred, 'Sebelius: Decrease in Human Beings Will Cover Cost of Contraception Mandate,' *Cybercast News Service*, 1 March 2012.

Lunn, Stephen and Lauren Wilson, 'Stop paying the Well-Off to Breed,' *The Australian* newspaper, 14 March 2008.

McElroy, Molly, 'Babies prefer fairness – but only if it benefits them – in choosing a playmate,' *University of Washington*, 14 April, 2014.

McKenny, Leesha, 'Catholic men better paid, says new study,' *The Sydney Morning Herald* newspaper, 15 November 2011, citing the *Applied Economics Letters* journal.

Messing, Philip with others, 'Cops scolded for mocking dive-bombing pigeon at G. Zero: sources,' *New York Post* newspaper, 10 December 2011.

Michael, Erin, 'Little white lies: Agnok Lueth adopts 'Daniel McClean' on his C.V. to try to get a fair go,' *mX* news at *News Limited Network*, 18 July 2011.

Moore, Tony, 'Rank racism: young Indian cabbies targeted,' *The Brisbane Times* newspaper, 8 May 2009. Michael Crutcher and Tuck Thompson, 'Indian taxi drivers hit back at critics,' *The Courier Mail* newspaper, 8 May 2009.

Morrison, Rob, 'Science shows we should get rid of 'race',' *The Punch*, 31 January 2011, with comment that day by Warren. Rob Morrison, ''Breakthrough' and other Swearwords: Science misbehaving in the Media,' *National Editors' Conference Papers*, Adelaide, 9 October 2009. Ethnicity and Genetics Working Group, National Human Genome Research Institute, Bethesda, 'The use of racial, ethnic and ancestral categories in human genetics research,' *American Journal of Human Genetics*, Volume 77, Issue 4, 2005. Morrison was a presenter of the *Curiosity Show* (1972-1990).

Moussaoui, Rana, 'Phoenician or Arab? A never-ending debate in Lebanon,' *The Sydney Morning Herald* newspaper, 8 June 2010.

Naik, Gautam, 'Switzerland's Green Power Revolution: Ethicists Ponder Plants' Rights,' *The Wall Street Journal* newspaper, 10

October 2008.

Noon, Chris, 'Buffett Will Double Gates Foundation's Spending,' *Forbes* magazine, 26 June 2006. 'How Are Asia's Entrepreneurs Preserving Their Family's Wealth?' *Union Bank of Switzerland*, 24 October 2013.

O'Loan, James, 'Rod Welford blames indigenous grades for low state average,' *The Courier Mail* newspaper, 22 September 2008.

Owen, Amy and others, 'Religious Factors and Hippocampal Atrophy in Late Life,' *Public Library of Science*, 2011. Leesha Mckenny, 'Religion may affect brain changes,' *The Sydney Morning Herald* newspaper, 23 May 2011.

Paine, Chris and Sarah Michael, 'LET'S MAKE A BABY: Mentos takes on Singapore's population crisis,' *News Limited Network*, 9 August 2012.

Passmore, Daryl, 'Adults only – Queensland's growing market for kids-free zones,' *The Sunday Mail* newspaper, 28 April 2002.

Ralph, Peter and Graham Coop, 'The Geography of Recent Genetic Ancestry across Europe,' *Public Library of Science Journal of Biology*, 7 May 2013. Eryn Brown, 'Everyone on Earth is related to everyone else, D.N.A. shows,' *Los Angeles Times* newspaper, 7 May 2013.

Ryder, Richard, 'All beings that feel pain deserve human rights: Equality of the species is the logical conclusion of post-Darwin morality,' *The Guardian* newspaper, 6 August 2005.

Sample, Ian, 'Whales and dolphins 'should have legal rights',' *The Guardian* newspaper, 21 February 2012. Uncredited, 'US judge asked to rule on orca 'slaves',' *Associated Press* news service published at *The Sydney Morning Herald* newspaper, 7 February 2012.

Schubert, Misha, 'Government to apologise for forced adoptions,' *The Sydney Morning Herald* newspaper, 23 June 2012. John Dagge, 'Sorry for 30-year adoption policy,' *Sunday Herald Sun* newspaper, 23 June 2012. Milanda Rout, 'Abbott heckled for 'offensive' terms at forced adoption apology,' *The Australian* newspaper, 21 March 2013.

Sheppard, Noel, 'Oprah: Racists Have to Die for Racism to End,' *Newsbusters*, 15 November 2013.

Snow, Deborah, 'Sandilands hits new low and ethnic council sizes up cause to complain,' *The Sydney Morning Herald* newspaper, 24 April 2010. Brian Browdie, 'Chinese condoms too small for

South Africa, judge rules in country most-affected by H.I.V./AIDS,' *New York Daily News* newspaper, 17 September 2011.

Swarns, Rachel, 'For Asian-American Couples, a Tie That Binds,' *The New York Times* newspaper, 30 March 2012.

Tanner, Lindsay, 2008 Redmond Barry Lecture, *State Library of Victoria.*

Taylor, Lee, 'Mike Mike creates Mr and Mrs Australia for Face of Tomorrow,' *News Limited Network*, 11 February 2011.

Thom, Greg, 'What does your mobile phone say about you?' *Herald Sun* newspaper, 18 September 2010.

Tonkin, Sam, 'More than 70% of doctors struck off in Britain are trained abroad: Alarm over patient safety despite promises to overhaul competency exams three years ago,' *Daily Mail* newspaper, 2 January 2016.

Tran, Mark, 'Invasion of the American lobsters: Sweden asks E.U. for help,' *The Guardian* newspaper, 19 March 2016.

Ujikane, Keiko and Kyoko Shimodoi, 'Abe Funds Japan's Last-Chance Saloon to Arrest Drop in Births,' *Bloomberg* news service, 19 March 2014.

Uncredited, 'American couples on trial in Egypt for adoption,' *Associated Press* news service published in *The Sydney Morning Herald* newspaper, 17 May 2009.

Uncredited, 'Aussies abroad: liked, but loud,' *The Sydney Morning Herald* newspaper, 9 July 2009.

Uncredited, 'A.Z. Dem Gubernatorial Candidate Darkens Skin for Commercials to Appear Hispanic,' *Breitbart News*, 5 August 2013, concerning Fred DuVal.

Uncredited, 'Blondes 'to die out in 200 years',' *British Broadcasting Corporation News*, 27 September 2002. Lawrence Altman, 'Hair-raising story about blonds cut short,' *The New York Times* newspaper, 3 October 2002.

Uncredited, 'British woman saves dogs from burning home – but forgets her grandchild,' *News Core* news service quoting *The Coventry Telegraph* newspaper, 9 June 2010.

Uncredited, 'Cherokee Indians: We are free to oust blacks,' *Reuters* news service published at *Microsoft National Broadcasting Company News*, 14 September 2011. James Dao with Ian Lovett, 'In California, Indian Tribes With Casino Money Cast Off Members,' *The New York Times* newspaper, 12 December 2011.

Uncredited, 'China arranging child adoptions' and 'China swamped with adoption offers,' *Agence France-Presse* news service, 16 May 2008.

Uncredited, 'City of cultures,' *The Sydney Morning Herald* newspaper 23 December 2011.

Uncredited, 'Dolls, and the guys paid to study them,' *The Australian* newspaper, 2 April 2003.

Uncredited, 'Eat your toast – or lose your virginity,' *Agence France-Presse* news service published at *News Limited Network*, 26 December 2008.

Uncredited, 'Experts concerned scientific advances are giving rise to neoracism,' *Agence France-Presse* news service published at *News Limited Network*, 15 February 2014.

Uncredited, 'Florida Passes Plan For Racially-Based Academic Goals,' *Columbia Broadcasting System Tampa* television news, 12 October 2012, citing the *Palm Beach Post* newspaper.

Uncredited, 'German ad promotes use of condoms with Mao Zedong, Adolf Hitler and Osama bin laden,' *Agence France-Presse* news service, 18 April 2009.

Uncredited, 'Gingers extinct in 100 years, say scientists,' *Daily Mail* newspaper (reporting an article in *National Geographic* magazine) published in *The Courier-Mail* newspaper, 23 August, 2007.

Uncredited, 'Hair salon had to remove job ad for 'happy' stylist because it is 'discriminatory' against unhappy people,' *Fox News*, 4 September 2020.

Uncredited, 'Miss Fiji row: 'She doesn't look native enough',' *The Daily Telegraph* newspaper, 27 April 2012. Michael Field, 'Fijian beauty queen loses crown,' *Fairfax New Zealand*, 13 May 2012.

Uncredited, 'Miss India not Indian enough,' the *New Zealand Herald* published at *The Sydney Morning Herald* newspaper, 14 October 2010.

Uncredited, 'Public servant on the run 'a naughty boy',' *The Sydney Morning Herald* newspaper, 11 December 2011.

Uncredited, 'Queen of the Hill,' *Teen People* magazine, May 1999. 'The Miselucidation of Lauryn Hill,' *Snopes* website.

Uncredited, "Reliable' worker ad discriminates against the unreliable,' *The Telegraph* newspaper, 28 January 2010.

Uncredited, 'Strangers can spot 'kindness' gene: study,' *Agence France-Presse* news service published at *Yahoo! News*, 15 November 2011. Aleksandr Kogan and Sarina Rodrigues

Saturn's results were published in the *Proceedings of the National Academy of Sciences*, 14 November 2011.

Uncredited, 'Victim of multimillion-dollar swindle embarks on a quest for justice,' *The Sydney Morning Herald* newspaper, 23 January 2012.

Uncredited correspondents in Seoul, 'Mass blind date to help area's birth rate,' *Australian Associated Press* news service published at *News Limited Network*, 13 November 2009. Uncredited, 'Lights go out to make more babies,' *Agence France-Presse* news service published in *The Sydney Morning Herald* newspaper, 20 January 2010. Uncredited, 'Cut overtime, make more babies: S Korea,' *The Sydney Morning Herald* newspaper, 9 June 2010.

van Ree, Erik, 'Marx and Engels's theory of history: making sense of the race factor,' *Journal of Political Ideologies*, Volume 24, Issue 1, 4 December 2018.

Walsh, Christopher, 'Senator Nova Peris sought taxpayers' money to help her to carry out a 'freaky' extra-marital sexual tryst with Olympic medallist Ato Boldon,' *Northern Territory News*, 29 October 2014.

Whish-Wilson, Peter, 'The real reason behind the whaling backflip,' *The Drum* at *Australian Broadcasting Corporation News*, 10 January 2014.

White, Alex, 'Marriage breeds better children,' *Herald Sun* newspaper, 16 November 2011.

Wilkinson, Steve, 'We're wary of the hairy,' *The Sydney Morning Herald* newspaper, 24 February 2010.

Winslow, Olivia, 'Census report sees minorities becoming majority by 2042,' *Newsday*, 13 August 2008. Martin Cantor. 'White Americans no longer a majority by 2042,' *My Way*, 14 August 2008. Hope Yen, 'Census shows whites lose US majority among babies,' *My Way*, 23 June 2011. Hope Yen, 'Census: White majority in U.S. gone by 2043,' *Associated Press* news service published at *United States News on National Broadcasting Company News*, 13 June 2013. Caroline May, 'Census: More Minority Children Than Whites, More Whites Dying Than Being Born,' *Breitbart News*, 25 Jun 2015.

Zayan, Jailan, 'Egypt to strip men married to Israelis of citizenship' (also published as 'Egypt's men warned off marrying Israelis'), *Agence France-Presse* news service published at *Yahoo! News*, 5 June 2010.

Zolfagharifard, Ellie and Victoria Woollaston, 'Could robots turn people into PETS? Elon Musk claims artificial intelligence will treat humans like 'Labradors',' *Daily Mail* newspaper, 26 March 2015.

Books

Chua, Amy, born 1962, and Jed Rubenfeld, *Triple Package Culture* (2014), Penguin Press. Maureen Callahan, 'Tiger Mom: Some races are just better,' *New York Post* newspaper, 4 January 2014.

Darwin, Charles, 1809-1882, *On the Origin of Species* (1959).

Galton, Sir Francis, 1822-1911, *Hereditary Genius* (1869) and *Inquiries into Human Faculty and its Development* (1883). Russell Grigg, 'Eugenics...death of the defenceless,' *Creation* magazine, Volume 28, Number 1, December 2005-February 2006.

Joyce, Kathryn, *The Child Catchers: Rescue, Trafficking and the New Gospel of* Adoption (2012), Public Affairs. Chloe Angyal, 'Adoption trafficking,' *Daily Life*, 13 May 2013, cited a 2009 survey finding only homosexuals are more reviled than unwed mothers in South Korea. Uncredited, 'Secrets and lies in the histories of overseas babies,' *The Sydney Morning Herald* newspaper, 26 November 2012.

Hamann, Brigitte, translated by Thomas Thornton, *Hitler's Vienna: A Portrait of the Tyrant as a Young Man* (1999, 2010), Tauris Parke Paperbacks. Richard Evans, 'How the First World War shaped Hitler,' *The Globe and Mail* newspaper, 22 June 2011.

Hitler, Adolf, 1889-1945, *Mein Kampf*, translated into English by James Murphy, died 1946.

Kühne, Thomas, 2010, *Belonging and Genocide: Hitler's Community*, 1918–1945, Yale University Press, concerning Bruno Müller.

Lemkin, Raphae, 1900-1959, *Axis Rule in Occupied Europe: Laws of Occupation - Analysis of Government – Proposals for Redress* (1944).

Lynott, Douglas, *Josef Mengele*. Mengele lived from 1911 to 1979.

Miller, Alice, 1923-2010, *For Your Own Good (Am Anfang war Erziehung*, 1980). Allan Hall, 'Hitler's 39 living relatives revealed,' *The Sydney Morning Herald* newspaper, 15 September 2009. Heidi Blake, 'Hitler 'had Jewish and African roots,' DNA tests show,' *The Telegraph* newspaper, 24 August 2010.

Miller, Geoffrey, born 1965, *The Mating Mind: How Sexual Choice Shaped the Evolution of Human Nature* (2001). Miller responded to

'2013: What should we be worried about?' *Edge* website.

Moore, Michael, born 1954, *Stupid White Men…and Other Sorry Excuses for the State of the Nation!* (2001).

Murray, Charles, *The Bell Curve* (1994). Johann Hari, 'Andrew Sullivan: Thinking Out Loud,' *The Economist: Intelligent Life* magazine, Spring (13 April) 2009.

Owen, Jane Duncan, *Mixed Matches: Interracial Marriages in Australia* (2002), University of New South Wales Press, reviewed by Fiona A White, *Journal of Family Studies*. Katherine Feeney, 'When cultures clash,' *The Sydney Morning Herald* newspaper, 5 September 2012.

Sarrazin, Thilo, born 1945, *Germany Does Itself In* (2010). Uncredited, 'Mosques 'a feature of German landscape',' *The Sydney Morning Herald* newspaper, 18 September 2010. Oliver Lane, 'Germany To Lower Educational Standards For Benefit Of Migrants,' *Breitbart News*, 9 November 2015.

Singer, Peter, born 1946, *Animal Liberation* (1975).

Singer, Peter, born 1946, *Should the Baby Live* (1985).

Toland, John, *Adolf Hitler: The Definitive Biography* (1976) reported that the Nuremberg race laws exempted Adolf Hitler.

Wistrich, Robert, *Who's Who in Nazi Germany* (1997), Routledge, published at the *Jewish Virtual Library*, referred to Hitler's order of the destruction of Germany on 19 March 1945.

Films

Abyss, The (1989), written and directed by James Cameron.

Back To The Future (1985). Screenwriter Bob Gale spoke in *Back To The Future: Making The Trilogy* (2002).

Code Name: The Cleaner (2007). Sheila Roberts published her interview with Lucy Liu on *Movies Online*.

Funny Face (1956). Kay Thompson played Maggie Prescott. Leonard Gershe wrote the screenplay, for which he won a 1958 Academy Award.

General's Daughter, The (1999).

Girl Like Me, A (2005), a seven-minute documentary by Kiri Davis.

Hunted (1952).

Our Man in Havana (1959), written by Graham Greene (1904-1991). Alec Guinness played James Wormold.

Pelican Brief, The (1993).

Planet of the Apes (1968), *International Movie Database*.
Ratatouille (2007).
Shawshank Redemption, The (1994).
Spider-Man 3 (2007).
You Only Live Twice (1967). Welshman Roald Dahl, 1916-1990, wrote the screenplay. Englishman Ian Fleming, 1908-1964, wrote the book.

Judgments

Eatock v Bolt [2011] FCA 1103, Bromberg J's summary, 28 September 2011, Melbourne.
Loving v Virginia, 388 U.S. 1 (1967).
Pace v Alabama, 106 U.S. 583 (1883).
Perez v Lippold (known also as *Perez v Sharp*), 32 Cal. 2d 711, 198 P. 2d 17 (Cal. 1948).
Shaw v Wolf [1998] Indig LawB 49 and (1998) 4(12) Indigenous Law Bulletin 20. Margaret Simons, 'Bolt in court: freedom of speech v the prohibition of race hate writes,' *Crikey* website, 23 September 2010. Uncredited, 'Brandis 'alarmed' at medal for Bolt case lawyer,' *Australian Broadcasting Corporation News*, 14 February 2012.

Reports

McLachlan, Rosalie and others, 'Deep and Persistent Disadvantage in Australia,' *Productivity Commission Staff Working Paper overview*, July 2013. Natasha Bita, "Genes' a reason poor kids struggle at school, says government report,' *News Limited Network*, 10 July 2013.
National Children's Bureau, *Young People and Racial Justice*. Rosa Prince, 'Toddlers who dislike spicy food 'racist',' *The Telegraph* newspaper, 8 July 2008.
United Nations Educational, Scientific, and Cultural Organisation Publication 791 of 1950.

Songs

'My Generation' (1965), by Pete Townshend, born 1945, and performed by the Who.

'Times They Are A-Changin, The' (recorded 1963, released 1964), by Bob Dylan, born Robert Allen Zimmerman in 1941.
'Whiter Shade of Pale, A' (1967), music by Gary Brooker and Matthew Fisher, lyrics by Keith Reid, sung by English musical group Procol Harum.

Television Programmes

American Masters (1986 onwards), *Public Broadcasting Service*. Episode 1 of season 33 was titled 'Decoding Watson', broadcast on 2 January 2019.
Fugitive, The (1963-1967).
Inside the Actors Studio (1994 onwards), Bravo cable television channel. Episode 10 of season 6, broadcast on 20 August 2000, included an interview with Harrison Ford.
Proefkonijnen (Guinea Pigs), (21 December 2011), *Bart's News Network*. Uncredited, "Cannibal' TV presenters eat each other's flesh for Dutch show,' *News Limited Network*, 21 December 2011.
Race: The Power of an Illusion (2003), produced by Larry Adelman, *California Newsreel*. Noah Rosenberg and others, 'Genetic Structure of Human Populations,' *Science* magazine, Volume 298, Number 5602, 20 December 2002.
Sex and the City (1998-2004). Uncredited, 'Kristin Davis becomes a mum,' *The Sydney Morning Herald* newspaper, 10 October 2011.
Shire, The (2012). Anthony Sharwood, 'A triumph for the white, vacuous, botoxed minority,' *The Punch* website, 17 July 2012. Brittany Stack, 'Shire Tops Suburbs with Lowest Crime,' *The Sunday Telegraph* newspaper, 10 February 2013.
View, The (especially 29 July 2011), American Broadcasting Company. Sam Youngman, 'President Obama calls African-Americans a 'mongrel people',' *The Hill* website, 29 July 2010.

ABOUT THE AUTHOR

Simon Lennon has travelled throughout Europe, America, Australasia, Asia, and the South Pacific, seeing how similar European peoples are to each other (wherever we live) and how different we of the West are to everyone else. He has university bachelor's degrees in science and law and university master's degrees in commerce and business. He is married with six children.

His non-fiction collection *The West* comprises the following sixteen books:

Mending the West
The Unnatural West: An Overview
The Tribeless West: An Overview
The Homeless West: An Overview
The Vanishing West: An Overview

Individualism
Western Individualism
The End of Natural Selection
The Need for Nations

Identity
People's Identity: Race and Racism
Of Whom We're Born: Race and Family
Biological Us: Gender and Sexuality

Nationalism
A Land to Belong: Nationalism
The Failure of Multiculturalism

Cultures
Reclaiming Western Cultures
Christendom Lost
Aiding Islam

He is also the author of another non-fiction book, two collections of short stories, and five novels.

www.ingramcontent.com/pod-product-compliance
Lightning Source LLC
Chambersburg PA
CBHW020002290326
41935CB00007B/274